CAN YOU REALLY RETIRE A MILLIONAIRE WITH AN IRA?

Ever since Individual Retirement Accounts became available, savers and investors have been playing in a whole new ball park. Now there's one clear-headed, straightforward guide that answers your questions, spells out the rules of the new game, and tells you how to play—to win.

- What four types of people should *not* open IRAs?
- Why are IRAs replacing pension funds as America's favorite fiscal umbrella?
- How can they lessen your tax bite—even after you start drawing interest on them?
- Why does money you save in an IRA grow faster than money you save in a similar non-IRA account?
- What are the rules for IRA investments and what kinds of penalties can be imposed if you don't follow them?
- What's the best plan for you?

THE ABCs OF IRAs

"The kind of commonsense primer that every investor needs. Grace favors his readers with two qualities rarely combined in an investment book—clear writing and clear logic."—The Washingtonian

"Grace really has his act together . . . [He] helps you wade through the conflicting—and often inflated—claims."—The Philadelphia Daily News

THE ABCs OF

IRAs

The Complete Guide to
Individual Retirement Accounts

THE #1 INVESTMENT STRATEGY
OF THE EIGHTIES

by
WILLIAM J. GRACE, JR.

A DELL TRADE PAPERBACK

A DELL TRADE PAPERBACK

Published by
Dell Publishing Co., Inc.
1 Dag Hammarskjold Plaza
New York, New York 10017

One previous edition
New revised edition
First printing—January 1984

Library of Congress Cataloging in Publication Data

Grace, William J., Jr.
  The ABCs of IRAs.

  1. Individual retirement accounts—Handbooks, manuals, etc. I. Title. II. Title: ABCs of IRAs.
HG1660.A3G68 1982   332.024'01   82-12996
ISBN 0-440-50398-1

CONTENTS

5

Acknowledgments

I would like to express my humble thanks to the following people who helped make this book possible: Wayne Nelson for his tremendous influence on my career; Rafe Sagalyn and Peter Guzzardi for their vision of the book; Valerie Ruebush, Susan Grace Galassi, and Jonathan Galassi for continued encouragement; and Mary Feeley Grace, who first spurred my interest in writing.

Don't Be the Only Nonmillionaire in the Old Folks' Home

The subject of Individual Retirement Accounts (IRAs) is important for three reasons:

1. Our entire national economy can be affected by the success or failure of the new IRA program. Until recently, the rate at which Americans save money had dwindled and become one of the lowest of all the industrial nations. The Reagan administration has been trying to reverse this trend through the use of tax incentives, which it hopes will substantially increase the nation's depleted savings and restore the economy by providing funds to finance capital investment.

2. One of the nation's largest and most important industries—the savings and loan business—was devastated by high interest rates and the outflow of deposits between 1979 and 1982. Failures in this industry could cost billions of dollars and affect every taxpayer in the country. The cry for help from both banks and S & Ls was at least partially answered in the 1981 tax act's liberalization of IRAs, which traditionally have benefited the savings institutions more than the other financial companies.

3. The average American worker cannot afford to retire today. After years of rampant inflation, coupled with a totally inadequate retirement system, most older people in this country fear their retirement days—for good reason. Today only about one out of four people over sixty-five years old is getting any pension income at all other than Social Security.

There is no question about the importance of working toward self-sufficiency for your retirement years. It's not a matter of getting rich; it's a question of survival.

The IRA advertisers entice us with the promise of our becoming millionaires, but this may not be any great achievement in your lifetime. Consider this: A

13

million dollars thirty-five years from now will be the equivalent of just $50,000 today, based on an annual inflation rate of 10 percent between now and then. How much retirement income would $50,000 provide today? Chances are that being a millionaire may become simply a minimum financial standard a lot sooner than thirty-five years from now.

IRAs were never meant to be the answer to your financial worries. But they are an important supplement to retirement planning for most people. They have become immensely popular this year, now that every working person is suddenly eligible to own one. Their popularity and importance are not surprising, since IRAs have to do with two of the greatest concerns in modern American life: *taxes* and *old age*.

Everyone hates to pay taxes. An IRA plan offers a $2,000 deduction with no risk (depending on your plan). That means a net savings of $500 to $1,000 a year for taxpayers in the 25 to 50 percent brackets. Earnings from this account won't be taxed until retirement.

Most people are worried about their later years in life and doubt that they will have enough money to live comfortably. More and more people distrust the Social Security system, fearing that it will be bankrupt by the time they retire.

IRA plans, according to much of the recent advertising, promise participants a way to "get rich." Despite the devastating effects of inflation and eventual taxes, it is true that $4,000 a year contributed by a working couple for thirty years (say, from age 35 to 65), with an average yield of 10 percent, does compound to a million dollars when under the protection of a tax-deferred IRA plan.

Continued high interest rates have made IRAs even more attractive. While banks and S & Ls were strictly limited by what they could pay on other types of savings deposits until recently, all financial institutions have been allowed to pay whatever rates they want on IRA accounts since 1982.

Never has there been an investment opportunity so widely appealing, yet so confusing for most people, as the new IRAs. With last year's sudden eligibility of 100 million people, most of whom have never made an investment of any sort before, there is a crying need for a simple yet comprehensive guide to the subject.

There is a bewildering array of choices to be made when picking an IRA plan. Not only do you have to choose from among several different financial institutions that act as custodians, but within each plan there are endless varieties of specific investment vehicles. The risks, conditions, and expenses of each plan and each investment are different.

The recent advertising blitz has not made the decision easier for most investors. The new IRAs have ignited one of the fiercest marketing battles in financial history for the American worker's savings.

If you are considering spending $2,000 or more a year on a retirement plan for the rest of your life, it is extremely important to make a knowledgeable decision about which plan is best for you from the beginning. The purpose of this book is to give you enough background and comparative information to make that decision.

The book is brief, straightforward, easy to understand, and very objective. Every advantage and disadvantage of each plan is clearly spelled out. Although there is no best plan for everyone, of course, I do recommend certain types of plans for certain types of investors.

The book is divided into four sections. Section I covers a lot of the background information having to do with the subject of IRAs: what's wrong with our retirement system, why our economy needs a massive infusion of fresh investment capital, why all those financial institutions want your $2,000 so badly (and who the companies are), the desperate condition of the depository institutions today, and who should (or should not) start an IRA.

If you bought this book strictly as an investment guide and don't care about the peripheral subjects, you can start with Section II, which tells you exactly how an IRA works. It covers all the rules and procedures that you will need to know, regardless of what type of plan you choose.

Section III is the most important part of the book. Here you will find a comprehensive comparison of what is offered by each of the main financial institutions that act as IRA custodians: depository institutions (banks, S & Ls, credit unions), brokerage firms (which offer self-directed plans), mutual fund companies, and insurance companies. The important thing to keep in mind when reading this section is that your choice of an IRA plan is an *investment decision;* and here the book becomes an investment guide as well as an IRA guide. An IRA *plan*, remember, has to do with just the account itself. What distinguishes the various accounts that are being offered by the IRA sponsors are the specific investment choices in those accounts.

The last section of this book contains every question you ever had about IRAs but didn't know whom to ask. Although this book is divided into four subject categories, be aware that many of the topics overlap. If you are using this section as a reference for a specific question, try different subjects that it may fall under.

Spending a single evening with this book could be one of the best investments of time and money you will ever make. I hope you will find it easy to read yet comprehensive enough to answer any question you could have on the subject of IRAs. Enjoy it!

Why Are IRAs
So Important?

1

Inadequacies of the System

In most languages there is no word for what we call "retirement," and in most societies little is provided for people who are too old to work.

Eskimos, we are told, sent their elderly off on icebergs when they were no longer able to work. Yet in America retirement is an institution. In this country some 30 million retired people are being serviced today by a gigantic industry and a governmental system that spends over $50 billion a year.

Americans have come to feel that they have a right to retire comfortably. In fact, a leisurely and financially worry-free retirement is one of our greatest goals. Most Americans spend three quarters of their lives enduring the drudgery of their work in hope that they can enjoy the last quarter doing things they had neither the time nor the money to do before. The Florida retirement communities, among other businesses, have done their part in keeping this Great American Dream alive for half a century.

But the reality of retirement for most people is not as happy as the dream. We have not seen the best of times in recent years in America. Crippling inflation, an inadequate pension system, and a nearly bankrupt Social Security system have dashed all hopes of making that dream come true for most people.

The Pension System

There is a general misconception in this country that most of our workers will receive pension benefits when they retire. A close look at the actual statistics, however, shows that only about 45 percent of all private-industry workers have any coverage by a company pension plan; and only 20 percent of all persons now retired are collecting benefits from a private pension. The pension industry itself is threatened by our ever-increasing life expectancies. As the number of retired people increases, the percentage of working people in the overall population decreases. The number of Americans over sixty-five years of age has grown from about 12 million in 1950 to over 24 million in 1980 and is expected to increase rapidly over the next ten years, while the total population remains relatively stable.

The whole idea of pension plans is relatively new. The tradition of industry had always been to retire older workers as soon as they became less productive or if they pose any threat to the safety or morale of the production line. A few companies rewarded loyal employees with small pensions in the early part of this century; and the early unions tried to establish retirement plans for members during these years. It was during World War II, however, that pensions became much more prevalent, because the government began to encourage private industry to offer them during this time. The unions' push for pensions took a giant step forward in 1948 after a Supreme Court decision that made pensions a legal bargaining condition of labor-contract negotiations.

Between 1948 and 1974 the number of companies that installed pension plans grew rapidly. But abuses were plentiful. It was not uncommon for long-time employees to find themselves being laid off shortly before retirement or to discover that they were ineligible for benefits because of some fine print in the original pension plan, after a lifetime of service. Workers also had no protection from mismanagement of either their pension plan or of the company itself. If the company invested its pension funds unwisely or mingled this money with their own operating funds, the employees could be left with no retirement money at all. Even worse, there was no protection of employee retirement funds in cases where companies actually went out of business.

The government had no real means of protecting employee benefits until the 1974 Employee Retirement Income Security Act (ERISA) which Congress passed only after years of debate on what to do about the growing problem of corporate pensions. But ERISA did do a lot to protect the rights of employees covered by pension plans. It set up standards for company funding and investing that would ensure that money does go into the plan each year, that it be invested prudently, and that pension funds always be segregated from the company's own money. The Pension Benefit Guarantee Corporation was also created by ERISA to protect the retiree from a company's inability to pay benefits that are due in cases of bankruptcy.

ERISA does not require companies to have a pension plan; it just regulates those that do. Unfortunately, ERISA does nothing to solve many of the problems that continue to plague the pension system today: (1) Not enough people are covered. (2) Most of those who are covered will never get their benefits. (3) Those that do actually receive benefits still will not have enough to live on adequately after retirement. The President's Commission on Pension Policy tells us that retired people need between 50 percent to 80 percent of their preretirement income after retirement; yet combined Social Security and pension benefits (if they even have a pension) usually fall considerably short of this.

It is unlikely that many new pension plans will be started in the future. The plans are very expensive to set up and administer, and the tax benefits that come with having a pension plan are now less significant because of the recent change in corporate tax rates. And labor unions, which traditionally played a major role in starting up corporate pension plans, will probably have less influence in the future because of their own lack of growth.

The reason that most people who are covered by a pension will never get paid is that they won't be at the same job long enough to become eligible for benefits. If you leave a company before becoming "vested" in its retirement plan, which usually takes about ten years, you walk away from whatever funds accumulated for you while you were there. A look at the statistics shows that even though 45 percent of private-industry workers are included in some pension plan, only about 25 percent of these workers are actually eligible for benefits at any given time.

The problem here is that people today change jobs more often than ever before. The average worker changes jobs well before reaching the minimum years for vesting. There is little chance that industry will shorten this vesting time, either. Shorter vesting periods would not only be very costly but would also reduce what little hold a corporation has over employees to keep them for a longer period of time.

Even if you actually get vested in a pension plan, chances are that you will be very disappointed by the amount of money that you will eventually receive. Average private retirement payments now amount to about $4,000 a year. Some companies have made small increases in benefits, but not nearly enough to keep up with the cost of living. The older the retiree gets, the less relative income he or she receives.

The message that this information conveys is loud and clear: Don't depend on a pension plan to support yourself during retirement. Your own resources, including an IRA plan, could become your only means of income in later life.

The Social Security System

Unfortunately you can't depend on the Social Security system any more than the pension system for your retirement years. Everyone has heard by this time that the Social Security system is in deep financial trouble; but I have found that most people don't really understand what the trouble is or even how the system works to begin with. Let's start with a little background on how the system works.

Social Security taxes are shared by you and your employer during your working years. The money collected goes into three trust funds, which are designated for specific purposes: the retirement fund (pays benefits to retirees), the health fund (Medicare), and the disability fund. The amount that you are taxed depends on your income, of course. The current rate is 6.7 percent of earnings, up to a maximum income of $32,400. Earnings above this "taxable wage base" are not taxed by Social Security.

Once you are part of the system, you or your dependents become eligible for benefits when you retire or if you become disabled or die. The money you contribute to the system, however, is not designated specifically for you. In this gigantic revolving door system, the money workers pay in is used for benefits being paid out to other people the same year.

The system was designed to allow for slightly more income than expenditures, so that excess funds could be held and invested (in Treasury bills) for each trust's reserve requirements. This plan worked well for many years. From the time Social Security levied its first tax

(1937) until the mid-1970s, the system enjoyed the comfort of reserve surpluses almost continually.

In the early 1970s three things happened that threw the Social Security system for a loop: (1) The unemployment rate started to rise, which reduced the system's income. (2) The inflation rate started to rise, which increased the system's expenses (benefits are tied to the cost of living). (3) In the great tradition of government bureaucracy, a gross miscalculation actually slipped by the Social Security Revisions of 1972 and got signed into law.

The slipup in Social Security arithmetic is an embarrassment in Washington to this day. The indexing formula that was passed into law would have eventually provided immense benefits to retirees, giving them more income than they had ever earned while working. How the mistake ever got by the Office of the Actuary, Congress, and the administration is still a mystery; but it was finally corrected five years later in the 1977 Social Security amendments.

While the government's bad math had no lasting effect on the Social Security system, the unemployment and inflation problems have grown worse. Last year the Social Security trustees told us that unless major steps were taken, the old age (retirement) and disability funds would be depleted by late 1983 and Medicare would be bankrupt between 1986 and 1991. The retirement fund alone was losing some $30,000 per minute by mid-year 1982. The cost-of-living benefit increases over the past five years have been a gigantic drain on the system's funds, and the current recession is reducing income rapidly due to even greater unemployment.

According to their 1982 annual report, the Social Security trustees (the Secretaries of Treasury, Health and Human Services, and Labor) say that Medicare is headed for disaster even if the economy strengthens significantly. Hospital costs have outrun the general pace of inflation by a wide margin. The old age and disability trusts, which paid out $156 billion in fiscal 1982, have even more immediate problems. The financial strength of these trusts is crucial to America's 36 million retirees, as two thirds of the nation's elderly depend on Social Security as their principal means of livelihood. Most experts agree that the longer-term prospects of the system's financial problems look even more dismal. Today's postwar "baby boom" generation will eventually swell the retirement ranks to an unsupportable worker/retiree ratio.

What to do about the Social Security problem is a tough political question. Do we increase taxes or reduce benefits? The American worker has already endured many tax increases for Social Security, and the current administration is philosophically opposed to tax increases of any type. Yet a reduction of benefits is unfair to the elderly and (as President Reagan found out in 1981) politically suicidal.

The uncertain future of Social Security underscores the importance of providing for yourself. Don't count on anyone else, especially the government, to do it for you. The IRA ad that displays a Social Security check stamped "Insufficient Funds" (and asks, "Will Social Security retire before you do?") may be using scare tactics, but it makes a good point. Your IRA account may not be just a supplement to Social Security, but perhaps the only reliable source of income in your retirement years.

Helping Yourself

The problem of limited retirement options goes back many years. Ever since pension plans started emerging after World War II, both the self-employed and those not covered by corporate plans have been trying to get the freedom to create their own retirement plans.

A major breakthrough took place in 1962 when Congressman Eugene J. Keogh was responsible for a new law that allowed the unincorporated self-employed to carry their own plans. The title of this act is designated as H.R. 10; and the new plans have been known as Keoghs ever since.

But Keogh plans covered only the self-employed. There were still millions of people who were employed by companies that just didn't have any retirement plan. It wasn't until the 1974 ERISA laws that IRAs were added for people not covered by either a pension or Keogh. Even though the amount of allowable contributions increased over the years (up to 15 percent of income with a maximum of $1,500 per year before the 1981 tax act), the use of IRAs remained surprisingly low. The President's Commission on Pension Policy found that in 1979 only about one out of twelve eligible people in the $10,000 to $50,000 income range took advantage of the IRA opportunity.

With every working person suddenly eligible for an IRA in 1982, the plans are expected to be much more popular. And the evolution of the individualized pension concept probably isn't through yet. Given the tradition of increasing the contribution limits on both IRAs and Keoghs (which just leaped from $7,500 to $30,000), most pension experts feel that the $2,000 IRA limit will be raised regularly over the years. Many economists expect the new IRAs to represent a whole philosophical change in America about encouraging savings by reducing taxes on interest and investment income.

There are several ideas being considered right now about how to make IRAs even more appealing in the future. One area of concern has to do with liquidity. While some economists propose eliminating the withdrawal penalties altogether, others propose special IRAs that can be tapped for particular reasons such as education or housing.

However they change in coming years, IRAs are

likely to become even more appealing than they are today. We have every reason to believe that they will be used more extensively as a means of restoring the nation's savings accounts and as a means of making American workers more self-sufficient in planning for their own retirement.

2

Reaganomics

Ronald Reagan was elected president by a landslide vote on November 4, 1980, because of his promise to save this country's devastated economy. His economic plan had four parts: monetary reform to fight inflation, regulatory reform to improve productivity, cutbacks in government spending to reduce the deficit, and tax reduction to spur economic growth.

In the first eight months of his presidency, Reagan succeeded in the enactment of the largest tax cut in history: the Economic Recovery Tax Act of 1981. With sweeping tax reductions for both individuals and corporations over a three-year period, the new tax law was based on the concept of recirculating badly needed private capital into the economy.

With the tax cuts came the government spending cuts, in almost every area except defense. The new President's promised experiment, at least with taxes and spending, had begun. But the real key to Reagan's economic program was his attempt to change the very faith of the American people: a transformation from a nation of spenders into a nation of savers. For a dozen years consumers were rewarded for spending and borrowing money. With interest rates low and inflation rates high, the economics of debt couldn't have worked better than it did in the 1970s. Ask any veteran real estate investor who got in early during this period.

Until recently, people who saved money saw their assets shrink rapidly due to inflation and taxes. We became a nation of spenders, and our rate of savings dropped from 8 percent in 1970 to 4.6 percent by the early 1980s. (This rate is the second lowest of the world's major nations; Japan's, by comparison, is 19.5 percent.)

Now, with the inflation rate low and interest rates still relatively high, many are beginning to reap the benefits of saving rather than spending. The new tax bill offers a host of incentives to individual taxpayers in order to convince them to recirculate their extra money into the savings system. IRAs are the greatest incentive of all because they affect the largest number of people.

The savings plan is the mainstay of Reaganomics. By raising the nation's anemic savings rate, we hope to provide funds for capital investment that will spur economic growth and eventually reduce the federal deficit. Whether this program will really work is questionable, since the deficit is now so great that the government's own financing needs over the next few years may very well soak up the nation's excess savings funds. A by-product of this event would be the continuation of high interest rates.

The new "economics of savings" may or may not revitalize our suffering national economy, but it clearly offers individual investors an opportunity to spur their personal finances a little in the years to come. There were three important savings incentives in the 1981 tax bill that affect millions of people directly. The first was a unilateral 25 percent cut in tax rates over three years. This created an immediate increase of disposable income for everyone, although there is no assurance that this extra income will increase the savings rate. The second important benefit provided by the new tax bill affected only the highest-income people: the maximum tax on unearned income and capital gains was reduced from 70 percent to 50 percent, beginning in 1982. The maximum tax on long-term capital gains (investments held more than one year) was consequently reduced to only 20 percent. This means that higher-income people will now have more incentive to make investments that produce taxable income and capital gains.

The third big tax incentive to savers is by far the most universally appealing: the liberalization of IRAs. Any working person can now contribute to an IRA plan and deduct the entire amount from taxable income, deferring all earnings in the account until retirement. Some 100 million people were suddenly eligible for this tax gift. The Reagan strategy of savings may benefit more from the IRA plan than from anything else; some economists expect an eventual inflow of $50 billion a year to IRA plans (once the contribution limits are raised), which could increase our overall savings rate by about 30 percent over its presently depressed level.

3

Competition for Your IRA Dollars

The main purpose of this book is to help the novice investor make an intelligent decision about what type of IRA plan to use. Every plan is different. What you get when you walk into a brokerage office, for example, is very different from what you get when you walk into your local savings and loan institution.

Before you begin your comparison of the IRA plans themselves, it's important that you understand the financial institutions that are sponsoring these plans. I have found that most people don't really understand the differences among the various organizations that make up our overall financial system. What is the real difference, for example, between a bank and an S & L?

The traditional roles of these institutions are changing rapidly, as each industry begins to trespass on the long-respected turf of the others in the new age of deregulation. They are all competing for the same trillion dollars of today's consumer deposits. They all see the

31

new IRAs as one of the best opportunities ever to go after new money and to attract money away from their competitors.

The Savings Institutions

Let's take a look at the traditional roles of the various depository (savings) institutions before seeing how they started to fall victim to the great blending process that give rise to what are now known as financial supermarkets.

The following institutions all make money the same way: They borrow funds (take in deposits) at one rate of interest and lend funds out (mortgages, business and personal loans, etc.) at a higher rate of interest.

COMMERCIAL BANKS

The traditional role of commercial banks, which are also called trust companies, community banks, or just plain banks, is that of a short-term commercial and consumer lender.

Banks offer a multitude of services for borrowers and savers: checking and savings accounts, mortgage and consumer loans, unsecured installment loans, credit cards, and investment services such as trust departments and estate planning. In recent years electronic banking has helped modernize this old and conservative institution. Some banks cater to commercial business, while others specialize in the consumer trade.

Of the fifteen thousand commercial banks in this country, most are members of the Federal Reserve System and almost all are insured by the Federal Deposit Insurance Corporation (FDIC). They may be chartered by either federal or state government. Banking is still a tightly regulated industry, and until recently commercial banks were restricted to paying lower interest rates on savings than any of the other depository institutions. With recent liberalization of rates on some of their deposits, the banks hope to be much more competitive in the new IRA market.

SAVINGS AND LOAN ASSOCIATIONS

Commonly known as S & Ls, but sometimes still called cooperative banks, savings associations, building and loan, or even homestead, associations, the savings and loan associations are structurally very different from the commercial banks.

The tradition of the S & L is that of a cooperative organization for the purpose of offering home mortgages. People saving money to buy a home would have a place to deposit their savings where it would be safe and earning more interest than at a commercial bank. Those people ready to buy a home could then borrow money from the association (other members' savings) in the form of a long-term mortgage.

S & L savers become members of the association, and their deposits are actually shares of stock in the organization. Their earnings on savings are really dividends on shares, earned mostly from mortgage lending. When you withdraw money from an S & L, the S & L is really buying back your shares from you, since you are a stockholder rather than a creditor (which is what you are in a bank). Traditionally even the mortgage lending was done almost exclusively for members. The savers always outnumber the borrowers in such a system because of the size of the mortgages; the current rate of savers to borrowers in all S & Ls is about five to one.

Today S & Ls are offering more financial services, such as bill-paying services and interest-paying checking accounts (called NOW accounts). S & Ls have also been the clear leaders in IRA business since the inception of IRAs in 1975. The reason for this has been aggressive marketing and a combination of insured safety and slightly higher interest rates than the commercial banks offer. They hope to hold their lead in IRAs in this new era of open competition.

Like commercial banks, the nation's 4,200 S & Ls may be either federally or state chartered and either insured or uninsured. The federally chartered S & Ls must be insured by the Federal Savings and Loan Insurance Corporation (FSLIC). While most state-chartered associations are now FSLIC insured too, those that carry private insurance instead usually pay higher interest on deposits than the others.

Ever since World War II (until recently), the S & L business has been very profitable. The owners simply took in money at one rate and lent it out at a higher rate. But the recent era of high inflation and soaring interest rates has caught up with this industry and almost destroyed it. This problem is covered in detail in the discussion beginning on page 39.

CREDIT UNIONS

Like S & Ls, credit unions (CUs) are cooperative associations made up of members who become shareholders and receive dividends instead of interest. But unlike S & Ls, the credit unions are nonprofit organizations made up of members with a common bond (employment, profession, union, etc.) and traditionally serve the purpose of making small, short-term consumer loans rather than large, long-term mortgage loans. Since they deal only with individuals, are run by members, and are nonprofit, CUs have served the function of paying higher rates on savings and charging lower rates on loans than the other financial institutions.

Like banks and S & Ls, credit unions may be either federally or state chartered and most have their own federal insurance through the National Credit Union Administration. And like the other institutions, CUs are now expanding their financial services beyond their traditional roles and today are known to offer mortgages, credit cards, savings and checking accounts, and electronic banking services.

Although the CUs are not nearly as significant an institution as the banks and S & Ls, they too are now in the thick of the competition for your IRA dollars.

MUTUAL SAVINGS BANKS

The mutual savings banks make up an old institution in this country that has always been concentrated in the New England states. Although they are really banks and offer most of the commercial bank services, mutuals look like S & Ls structurally because they are owned by and operated for their depositors only. They generally pay a higher rate on savings than commercial banks and are governed only by state law. Since mutual savings banks hold a relatively small percentage of total consumer deposits, they are not considered a real factor in the IRA competition.

Financial Supermarkets

The blending together of the big financial institutions in the 1980s may be the most significant change in the way people handle their money since the invention of paper currency some eight hundred years ago.

Not only are the four depository institutions just described starting to look more and more alike as their traditional functions continue to overlap, but even financial institutions that were once considered unrelated are now competing against each other with the same products and services. The American consumer will soon find most financial service companies virtually indistinguishable and will probably go to a single company for almost anything that has to do with money.

The competition today between the new financial giants for cash deposits and new customers is more intense than ever, as each wants to establish itself as the most complete money company of the eighties. IRA accounts are just another way to attract money and people, but they happen to be the best product that these companies have had in some time. As the nation's biggest banks, insurance companies, brokerage firms, credit card companies, and even retail organizations clamor to be leaders in the financial industry, your $2,000 IRA account becomes a key target in their marketing efforts.

The goal of each of these giants—companies like Citicorp, American Express, Prudential, and Sears—is to become a one-stop money management company providing every conceivable financial service under the same roof. Three of these companies jumped into the securities business in 1981 by purchasing brokerage firms. Prudential, the nation's largest insurance company, also became the largest stockbroker when it added Bache Halsey Stuart to its vast financial distribution system. The $375 million purchase took less than two weeks to negotiate from beginning to end for the $60 billion Prudential. Just a month later two other financial leaders struck their own deal. American Express, the $24 billion travel, communications, international banking, and insurance conglomerate, added Shearson Loeb Rhoades to its inventory for $930 million and instantly became the second largest securities firm.

The third big financial purchase in 1981 was the most startling of all. Sears Roebuck, already a leader in the insurance (Allstate), savings and loan, and real estate industries, acquired both the nation's largest real estate firm and one of the largest securities firms within a period of just four days. With the addition of Coldwell Banker for $180 million and Dean Witter for $600 million, the $33 billion Sears organization instantly became the most complete, if not the largest, financial-service company of all.

up with new products such as money market funds, insurance annuities, and tax shelters to help hold its customer base. Today the industry actually derives a majority (two thirds) of its income from sources other than commissions of any kind. The brokers are starting to look more like bankers, much to the dismay of the real banks. The distinction between the two industries is becoming more unclear all the time. "In the future, I don't see why one of our customers would need a bank," says Dean Witter's chief financial officer, Thomas Schneider, in the May 4, 1981 issue of *U.S. News & World Report*. "The distinction between services provided today by banks and those provided by brokerage firms already has become blurred to some extent and will become even more so by the late 1980s."

The Plight of the S & Ls in the Early 1980s

We have looked at the savings institutions to get familiar with the companies that traditionally harbored the nation's IRA funds. And the new concept of diversified financial services shows us what intense competition there is right now for the new IRA customer.

But the most significant story behind the financial industry's lobby for the new IRAs lies in the desperate state of affairs that the nation's S & Ls were in at the time. In fact, the principal reason that Congress suddenly made every working person eligible for IRAs is that a generous measure was needed to help attract vast deposits to an industry that was in serious danger of falling apart. The S & Ls responded by becoming the toughest competitors for your IRA money, spending millions of dollars in an unprecedented advertising blitz in 1982 and 1983.

As money poured out of S & Ls and into money market funds in the 1979–1982 period, and as the cost of attracting new money remained high with interest rates, more and more S & Ls began losing money. In 1982, more than 60 percent of the nation's 4,200 S & Ls were operated at a loss, and as many as one third of them were seriously in danger of failing. Many doors closed in the industry, and hundreds of desperate mergers took place. Together, the S & Ls were losing $15 million a day for a while in 1982. The plight of this industry, which holds $500 billion in savings deposits, was beginning to look like one of the biggest financial disasters in American history.

The problem that all the depository institutions faced was a combination of high interest rates and government regulations that prevented them from competing in an open marketplace. The Banking Act of 1933 imposed the first restrictions on the interest rates that banks and thrifts (other savings institutions) could pay. The act was the result of the disorganized and unregulated banking industry's contribution to the Depression. A provision called Regulation Q gives the government the right to dictate interest rates paid by banks. This same act is what prevents banks and thrifts from operating in more than one state and, until recently, from paying any interest at all on checking accounts.

The Depository Institutions Deregulation and Monetary Control Act of 1980 made the first significant regulatory concessions since 1933. Savings institutions were allowed to pay 5¼ percent (hardly competitive with money market funds) on checking accounts (called NOW accounts), and the ceiling on savings account rates will be abolished by 1986.

The issue of interstate banking is even more important to the industry than the interest rate issue. Some banks are fully prepared for the eventuality of this freedom. Citicorp, often considered the most creative company in this banking industry, already has a network of 170 consumer finance offices all over the country. These could easily be converted to deposit-taking bank branches if and when the regulations are lifted. This same company, in the meantime, is coping with regulatory restrictions and competition through the use of innovative consumer marketing, such as the massive use of automated-teller machines and even the installation of home computer terminals with which customers can check their balances, pay their bills, or take out loans.

Banks as a group were never in nearly the trouble that the S & Ls were in, because banks traditionally make shorter-term loans at fluctuating interest rates. The S & Ls usually make long-term (mortgage) loans at fixed rates. While the interest being paid to the S & Ls was fixed at a very low rate (most were below 10 percent) for a long period of time (25 to 30 years), the interest being paid out by the same companies to attract new money today was very high. This is why almost all of them operated at a loss during the 1979–1982 period and why they have been eager to compete with other financial institutions for some of the more profitable financial business available today.

Although the problems of banks and S & Ls in this country were no laughing matter, the column by Art Buchwald from 1982, on pages 42 and 43, described the industry's woes in a simple and creative story.

A big lobbying victory for the S & Ls was demonstrated by two provisions of the 1981 tax act: the All Savers Certificate and the revision of IRA. Both of these tax allowances were passed to help the ailing S & L industry. Since the All Savers were planned for only one year, the IRA provision is by far the more important.

To save the S & Ls, the continued outflow of deposits must be stopped and the confidence of their customers must somehow be restored. In 1981 some 80 percent of the S & Ls had net operating losses as a staggering $39 billion of deposits flowed out to other institutions. Not all of it went to the higher-yielding money market funds either. Some $12 billion was transferred to commercial banks, which pay the same interest rate and are

Banking—Fund

By Art Buchwald

IF THERE has been any trickle-down effect from Reaganomics, it has been the crocodile tears of bankers and savings and loan managers who claim they are being creamed by high interest rates.

What most of them won't admit is that there are too many banks and S&Ls in this country in the first place. All you have to do is walk down any main street of America and you'll see one bank next to another, each oblivious to how many banks and savings institutions the traffic can stand.

"The trouble with the banking business," said Dartmouth, a down-and-out banker, "is that during the roaring '50s and '60s everyone and his brother went into it. It was a time when everyone else and his brother also went into the housing and commercial building business, and everyone and his sister became real estate agents.

"The people who didn't know anything about banking made loans to the people who didn't know anything about building, and for a while everyone considered themselves financial wizards. The word was out on the street that if you wanted to become J.P. Morgan all you had to do was find an empty ground-floor location and open a bank or an S&L. It was easier to get a charter for a bank than it was to get a driver's license, and before you knew it the nation was covered wall to wall with banks.

"Banks and S&Ls went all out to attract depositors. First they gave away Green Stamps. Then they offered dishes, heating pads, coffee grinders and electric toasters.

"As the competition got tougher they threw in television sets and trips to Disneyland, and they were happy to give you 5½ percent on your money, which they loaned out for 6½ percent to all of their friends.

"It was the golden age of banking and everyone thought it would last forever.

"Then came inflation, followed by unbelievable government deficits,

Capitol Punishment

followed by soaring interest rates, followed by Truesdale."

"Who's Truesdale?" I asked.

"He came up with a brainstorm and started the money fund business. He opened up a tiny office on the 30th floor of the Woolworth Building and began offering people 15 percent on their money instead of 5. Except for rent he had no overhead, and no employes. He didn't even have to put in a closed-circuit television system to watch his customers.

"People started taking their money out of banks and S&Ls and sending it to Truesdale. The gunslingers on Wall Street followed suit and soon there were as many money funds in the country as there were banks.

& Games

"At this moment the government had to go out and start borrowing money from the public to make up its deficits, and they had to pay as much interest as the money funds to make their notes attractive.

"So between the money funds and the U.S. Treasury, the banks and S&Ls couldn't compete for anyone's savings."

"That's a sad story," I said.

"What makes it even sadder is that when the interest rates went sky high, and the building industry went belly up, the banks and S&Ls were stuck with 6½ percent loans to everyone and his brother. No one could afford to borrow money for new housing, and the banks couldn't carry homeowners and developers at the old mortgage rates.

"To make matters worse every stockbroker and his brother is going into the banking business, and soon the department stores will be in it and supermarkets will open branches, and eventually a bank will have as much relevance to a town as a railroad station."

"I guess we won't see more banks and S&Ls opening in such a climate," I said.

"That's the funny part of it. Even now, every time you see a new building go up, the ground floor is always reserved for another bank."

"Why?" I asked.

"Because everyone and his brother still believes what bank robber Willie Sutton said: 'That's where the money is.' "

©1982, Los Angeles Times Syndicate

covered by the same type of federal insurance as the S & Ls. Many depositors simply feared having their money in a failing company, even though their deposits were fully insured.

Business did not seem likely to improve for the S & Ls in the early 1980s without a big decline in interest rates. The old mortgages that these companies held at such low rates were not apt to be turned over during the long housing slump. And the housing slump wouldn't improve if interest rates didn't fall. The circle of this frustration was completed by the irony that interest rates were remaining high because of the huge federal deficit, which would have gotten even worse if the government had to bail out the S & Ls.

As the thrifts' computers told them how much time they had left before they had to close their doors, the FSLIC was scrambling to arrange mergers within the industry. The trend was clear: 139 mergers in 1980, almost 300 in 1981, and well over 1,000 in 1982. The government began now encouraging interstate mergers and acquisitions. The stronger S & Ls, and even the stronger commercial banks, found themselves being asked to take over the weaker S & Ls in other states. This was the beginning of the bank's long-sought opportunity to make S & L acquisitions and to operate in a number of different states.

What really saved the S & L industry, of course, was a rapid decline in interest rates during the second half of 1982. The prime rate, which exceeded 20 percent in 1981, neared 10 percent by the end of 1982. Also in late 1982 the S & Ls finally got a chance to get back at the other financial institutions that had been draining money from the S & Ls for so long. The savings institutions, along with banks, were finally allowed to offer their own money market funds. Once again, aggressive advertising and above-market interest rates helped the depository industry gain on other financial companies in the new era of open competition.

4

Who Needs IRAs?

The experts all seem to agree that a working person has to be crazy not to take advantage of an IRA. Almost every major newspaper and business journal in the country has sung its praise for the new "tax shelter for everyone."

In its November 16, 1981 issue, *Fortune* magazine said, "Few well-paid taxpayers would dream of passing up the deduction available for setting away $2,000 in an Individual Retirement Account." And *Money* magazine said in February 1982 that an IRA is "the single most effective way to cut taxes this year."

Despite the almost universal appeal of IRAs, they are not for everyone. There are certain people for whom IRAs would not be a good investment plan: extremely high-income earners; people with very low, volatile, or unpredictable incomes; and people who are already too close to retirement age to benefit from the plan. There are also certain alternatives for tax deferral and retirement planning available to some people that may make IRAs relatively unimportant: pension, profit-sharing, and Keogh plans for the self-employed; deferred-compensation or salary-reduction plans for the corporate employed, and tax-sheltered investments for those who can afford them.

There is just one income qualification for IRA eligibility: your earned income must equal or exceed your IRA contribution in the same tax year. Of the 100 million eligible workers, probably three quarters should take advantage of this opportunity. Designed to supplement Social Security and any other retirement plan a person might already have, the IRAs are ideally suited for young and middle-aged workers who have reliable and adequate income in addition to some liquid reserves.

The Argument Against IRAs

While almost everyone applauds the new IRAs as Congress' greatest gift to the American taxpayer, there are still some skeptics who point out the few unattractive qualities of the program. Most of the complaints that I have heard are unfounded: costs and safety factors, for example, apply to non-IRA accounts too. As in other investment accounts, you have a galaxy of choices when it comes to exactly which investment is best for your money.

There are, however, certain characteristics of IRAs that you should be aware of before starting up your plan.

A. *Tax Factors.* If you lose money with any investment made in a nonretirement account, Uncle Sam will absorb some of that loss for you. *Capital losses* can offset capital gains, or even be used to reduce your ordinary income. But with retirement accounts, including IRAs, there is no deduction for capital losses. Keep in mind, though, that you have already deducted the entire amount of the IRA contribution at the time it is made.

We are reminded that IRA capital *gains*, on the other hand, will eventually be taxed as ordinary income (the highest tax rate), while non-IRA gains are currently taxed at a reduced rate if the investment was held for more than twelve months (long-term capital gains). This is true, but is certainly not a reason to shy away from an IRA account. Consider this example: $2,000 of income invested in a non-IRA account must first be taxed. If the taxpayer is in a 40 percent bracket, for example, then he is left with only $1,200 to invest. If he eventually doubles his money through a long-term capital gain, he then will have $2,400 before capital gains taxes. In his bracket, our investor would pay $192 ($1,200 gain, 40 percent of which is taxable at his 40 percent bracket) long-term capital gains tax, leaving him with $2,208 for his next investment. But what would have happened if he had put that same $2,000 of income in an IRA account and made the very same investment? First of all, the entire $2,000 would have gone to work, since the 40 percent income tax would be deferred indefinitely. When this money doubled in value the investor would then have $4,000 available for his next venture since capital gains taxes too are deferred. Even if this investor were to retire and withdraw the entire $4,000 immediately, he would come out ahead: assuming the same 40 percent bracket, some $1,600 would be deleted from his $4,000 total, still leaving him with $2,400.

What good is deferring taxes (IRAs *defer*, not eliminate) if you have to pay them anyway? There are two big advantages in tax deferral. The first is that you have the use of your money longer. If you keep that money invested, the "time value" is very significant. The other advantage of tax deferral that applies particularly to retirement plans is the possibility of paying taxes when you are in a lower bracket (after you retire) than you are in now. While the time value of money has no argument, the future of your tax bracket is certainly unknown. The skeptics point out that tax brackets have traditionally increased over the years, and that a huge retirement savings would put you in the highest bracket during your retirement years anyway. This may be true, but the tax-deferred use of your money is still so significant that it doesn't really matter whether your bracket is lower in retirement or not.

B. *The Inflation Factor.* "A million dollars isn't what it used to be." There is no question that inflation (at any rate) will take its toll on our savings over the years. To have the equivalent of today's million dollars, you will need about *$23 million* 35 years from now (based on an inflation rate of 9 percent).

While the promise of being a millionaire in the future may be a question of definition, this really has little to do with whether or not you should use an IRA. The real question is this: How can you best save money for your retirement? If an IRA savings plan helps you accumulate more money than a non-IRA savings plan, then it's a help to you, whether it makes you a millionaire or not.

C. *The Liquidity Factors.* As will be emphasized throughout this book, IRAs are not for money that you think you will need to spend. There is a penalty for withdrawing money from your IRA before retirement, and you cannot borrow money against your IRA account. However, unless you withdraw your IRA money within the first few years, the tax benefits usually outweigh the penalties. You will find a comparison of an early withdrawal versus not using an IRA on page 67. My advice is to go ahead with an IRA as long as you feel that you probably won't need the money in the first five years.

D. *IRAs Are Not for Everyone.* There is no argument with this statement. The following section discusses several situations in which IRAs are inappropriate.

E. *There Are Better Plans Than IRAs.* There are better retirement plans for people who are fortunate enough to have them available. You will find several of them outlined in a following section. Keep in mind, however, that an IRA account can be used in addition to any other retirement plan that you might be eligible for.

Who Should *Not* Start One?

Since the majority of people interested in IRAs probably *should* start a plan this year, let's look at the various reasons one should probably *not* start an IRA:

1. Very High Income. A tax deduction that is limited to $2,000 a year is not of tremendous concern to someone who must shelter much larger amounts to reduce a tax bill. Traditional tax-sheltering investments such as real estate, oil and gas, and equipment leasing may give the investor who can afford the risk an opportunity for long-term capital appreciation while deferring taxation on larger amounts of income at the same time.

One of the basic appeals of IRAs is that the participant can defer income from high-bracket years (working years) to lower-bracket years (retirement years). But if you expect your income to remain in the highest tax bracket after you retire, then the benefits of IRA are somewhat diminished.

2. Very Low Income. Obviously not everyone can afford an IRA plan. Since an IRA is an illiquid account with a 10 percent penalty for withdrawal before age 59½, one should certainly have adequate cash reserves and a dependable income before even considering this plan. If your tax bracket is fairly low, neither the deductions nor the tax deferral from an IRA will be that important to you, anyway. If you are not sure what tax bracket you are in, refer to the tables on pages 63–65.

Special expenses in your future should be taken into consideration when you are weighing the benefits of an IRA plan. Large cash requirements for the purchase of a house or upcoming tuitions should be kept liquid outside of an IRA.

One important thing to remember, however, is that there are no minimum requirements for IRA contributions. Many participants will contribute varying amounts each year, perhaps skipping some years' contribution altogether.

Most tax advisers recommend going ahead with an IRA even if your financial situation is borderline. Their reasoning is that the initial tax savings at the time of the contributions should in most cases outweigh the taxes and 10 percent penalty you would incur if you have to withdraw money from the plan before retirement.

A word of investment advice here: If your personal liquidity is questionable, more attention should be used to maintain greater liquidity without your IRA plan. It would be a mistake, for example, to invest in a plan that has its own withdrawal penalties in addition to the standard IRS tax penalties. Investments to avoid here would include specific-term savings certificates (certificates of deposit, called CDs) and insurance annuities. More about these on pages 92 and 147 respectively.

3. Age Factors. In its February 15, 1982 issue, *Forbes* magazine says, ". . . even if you are in your 50s, an IRA plan is the greatest thing to happen to potential retirees since the Sunbelt." Because the age limit for making contributions to an IRA is 70½, you can legally start a plan anytime before that (as long as you are still working).

From an investment adviser's point of view, however, few people beyond the age of 60 will benefit much by beginning an IRA. It takes quite a number of years to build a retirement nest egg at $2,000 a year. If you are a working person nearing retirement, you should figure out whether your tax bracket will be any lower after retirement than it is currently. If you have sizable investment income and more than adequate retirement plans, you may find that deferring current earned income for a few years into retirement income makes very little difference.

The same caution about liquidity should be stressed for older IRA investors as for lower-income people.

4. Some Self-Employed Individuals. Self-employed people often have very different financial requirements from other workers. If you are self-employed your income is apt to be more volatile, your earnings may best be invested back into your own business, and your retirement income may already be provided for through a Keogh plan or pension plan.

Highly volatile incomes are not very compatible with an IRA plan. In low-income years you may not want to tie up money in a lifelong plan and may even need to get previously invested money out of the plan. In high-income years, however, you may find that you need more tax shelter and must look for larger investments outside your IRA plan. IRAs are best suited for people with adequate and dependable incomes over a long period of time.

What's Better Than IRAs?

KEOGH

Keogh plans are similar to IRAs in many ways but are available only to self-employed workers. The maximum annual contribution for Keoghs is now $30,000 or 25 percent of earnings. Since using this plan does not preclude the use of IRAs too, a self-employed couple could deduct up to a total of $64,000 if each person contributes the maximum to both plans.

INCORPORATION

Those self-employed workers who choose to incorporate also have good opportunities to shelter income.

Like the Keogh plan, a corporate pension plan is limited by 25 percent of earnings up to $30,000.

Even though 1982 tax changes reduced some of the benefits of incorporation, the "closely held corporation" or "professional corporation" still provides perhaps the best overall tax benefits for self-employed people. If you follow the IRS's own rules, your shelter will not be questioned. After establishing a corporate retirement plan, the owner is given surprising leniency in juggling funds from corporate ownership to pension plan ownership to individual ownership.

Corporate contributions to your pension plan are tax deductible to the corporation and tax sheltered for you. When you retire or dissolve the corporation, you just roll your pension funds into an IRA plan to keep them sheltered. If you die, your spouse receives the pension money without paying inheritance tax.

Besides the pension plan tax advantages, the small corporation is also famous for its extensive insurance benefits: tax deductible to the corporation, of course, yet not taxable to the individual as income. Such benefits can include key-man insurance, disability, group health, and group life insurance (up to $50,000 tax free for a professional corporation).

Naturally incorporation is immensely popular for younger professionals today. The IRS gave up its long struggle to treat individuals who incorporate differently from larger corporations in 1970. Within a few years, the statistics show, over one third of the physicians in the United States had incorporated. Today more than half are incorporated although this number may change because of tax laws that affect professional corporations.

SALARY-REDUCTION PLANS

The hottest thing in tax deferrals for some people this year is not IRA but another scheme called a "salary-reduction plan."

Made possible by a provision of the tax act of 1978, the IRS just recently got around to issuing proposed regulations clarifying this provision. Under this plan a corporation can offer all its employees a chance to defer up to 10 percent of their earnings until they reach age 59½. The money, of course, is invested in the meantime; most plans will offer the participants various investment options. Many major corporations are already prepared to offer this tax-deferral plan.

A salary-reduction plan has several advantages over an IRA. With deferrals allowable up to 10 percent of earnings, this can mean a significantly larger tax deduction than an IRA for participants with salaries over $20,000. This plan, incidentally, can be used in addition to an IRA.

The salary-reduction plan is also a more complete tax shelter than the IRA. While contributions to an IRA plan will reduce federal taxes, you may still have to pay state tax (and always Social Security tax) on this amount. While an IRA contribution is made with money already paid to the worker, the salary-reduction plan is simply a reduction of the amount of income the employee receives and therefore no taxes at all are withheld on the deferred amount.

Like an IRA, dividends, interest, and capital gains earned with deferred money are also tax sheltered until they are withdrawn. But, unlike an IRA, this new plan has still more tax advantages when the lump sum is finally distributed at age 59½. While IRA distributions are taxed at the ordinary income rate, salary-reduction distributions qualify for a much more favorable tax treatment called "ten-year-forward averaging."

Possible liquidity is another major provision of the salary-reduction plan. Workers who need to withdraw funds for loosely defined "hardship" reasons (such as medical bills, tuition, or even to purchase a house) may do so without incurring a penalty. The early-withdrawal penalty for IRAs, you'll remember, is 10 percent, no matter what the reason.

Still another feature of the salary-reduction plans that will make them irresistible for many corporate employees is that many companies are planning to match contributions by adding twenty-five to fifty cents for every dollar the employee puts in. The company saves some money with this deferred-pay plan, because the plan reduces the amount of Social Security, unemployment insurance, workmen's compensation, and other expenses the company would otherwise incur on every dollar of salary actually paid out to employees. Deferred pay, however, is still a tax-deductible expense for the company. It is estimated that companies will save about ten cents for every dollar that is deferred through the new salary-reduction plan.

Honeywell was the first major corporation to initiate this new plan, starting the program on January 1, 1982. Already a huge success, the salary-reduction plan has been chosen by twice as many employees as have chosen the company's IRA plan, which also began on January 1. Many other corporations will begin salary-reduction plans this year. Because of their many advantages over IRAs, they will no doubt be more popular for workers who have the opportunity to participate in them. Check with your company to see if it plans to initiate this program.

DEFERRED COMPENSATION

Many of the larger corporations now offer their highest paid executives a plan that beats every other tax shelter; there is no limit on how much money can be protected. A "nonqualified deferred compensation" plan is simply a withholding of a portion of the executive's earned income by the corporation until the employee retires or leaves the company. Since there is no limit on the amount that may be deferred, some executives now shelter a large percentage of their total compensation in this type of plan.

The funds that are deferred are legally owed to the employee, who becomes a creditor of the corporation. Such plans have been especially popular in recent years of high interest rates, because the corporation generally pays interest on this money at approximately the prime rate. No taxes are due on either the original earnings or the accumulated interest until the employee actually starts receiving the money. The distribution can be spread out over many years or taken as a lump sum when the executive leaves the company.

IRAs and Women

A sixty-five-year-old woman is expected to live about 30 percent longer than a sixty-five-year-old man. Even though women are more apt to need pension benefits during their retirement years, statistics show that women are much less covered by pension plans than are men.

Women who outlive their husbands—and most women do—often get no benefits from their husbands' pensions. A surviving widow receives benefits only in a plan that has been previously designated for a special type of annuity option by her husband.

Statistics continue to show that considerably lower lifetime earnings for most women result in less than adequate retirement benefits from both Social Security and pensions, even for women who do get vested in a company plan. The relationship between pensions and Social Security, incidentally, represents another absurdity in the question of women's retirement benefits. There is a pension rule called "integration" that allows a company to reduce or even eliminate pension benefits for lower-income vested workers based on a formula that takes into consideration the Social Security payments that these workers will eventually receive.

The two major problems with the private pension system that affect women considerably more than men in this country are the questions of pension *coverage* and the question of pension *benefits* (becoming vested).

Since there is no regulatory requirement for a pension plan to cover workers under age twenty-five, many young working women are at an immediate disadvantage: the highest employment rate for women occurs in the under-twenty-five age group. The percentage of working men covered by private pensions in this same group is 65 percent greater than the percentage of working women covered. In the over-twenty-five age group the percentage of male coverage is still 55 percent greater. These figures are partly a result of the fact that large numbers of women work in jobs that have no pension plans at all.

Even for workers who *are* covered by pension plans, getting vested in a plan has traditionally been more difficult for women than for men. If a woman leaves her job and returns several years later, as many women do, her original years of work often are not credited toward the requirements of her company's retirement plan.

All the facts confirm the importance of individual retirement planning for women: women live a lot longer than men, yet earn a lot less money and receive a lot fewer retirement benefits than men. While these conditions may be slowly changing, good advice to women today is to pay particular attention to providing for their own retirement. IRAs are probably more important for women than for men because of the general lack of other retirement funds for women. IRAs do not discriminate against job status, income, longevity, or other retirement plans.

SECTION II

How IRAs Work

5

General
Procedures

It is no mystery why IRAs are so popular. They are at
least a partial answer to two of our greatest concerns:
taxes and *old age*. Simply put, an IRA allows you to
defer current income, and therefore income taxes, until
you retire. Even though you will eventually have to pay
the tax on your IRA funds, there are four good reasons
to take advantage of this do-it-yourself retirement plan.
(1) The current tax deduction alone can mean a net
savings of up to $1,000 per year per person. (2) Tax-
deferred money grows at a much faster rate than after-
tax money (just look at the table that follows). (3) Most
people will be in a lower tax bracket after they retire
than they are in during their working years. (4) An IRA
plan forces you to save money.

This chapter will tell you how an IRA works and
what the general rules and procedures are for owning
one. You may want to refer to Section IV for specific
questions about the topics covered here.

What a difference an IRA makes

These three stacks of money illustrate the dramatic boost an IRA tax shelter can give retirement savings. Each stack represents the eventual nest egg for an investor who sets aside $2,000 of pretax income at the beginning of each year for up to 40 years. It is assumed that the money earns 10% interest each year, compounded annually.

* The largest stack of bills represents results for an IRA in which the full $2,000 is invested and earnings accumulate tax-free.

* The middle stack represents results for a taxpayer without an IRA whose income is taxed at a 25% rate. Only $1,500 is available for investment after taxes, and each year 25% of the earnings must be turned over to the IRS. In reality, it is doubtful that anyone would remain in the same tax bracket for 40 years. Changes in income and in the tax laws are likely to cause the rate at which income is taxed to fluctuate, perhaps significantly.

* The smallest stack represents results for someone without an IRA who faces a 50% tax bill. This person's after-tax annual contribution is $1,000, and half of the annual earnings go to pay taxes.

To see what an IRA can mean in terms of added retirement income, assume that the cash accumulated over 40 years were withdrawn in annual installments over a 20-year period, during which the balance of each account continued to earn 10%. The IRA owner would get $103,974 at the beginning of each year; the non-IRA saver in the 25% bracket would get $39,130; the one in the 50% bracket a relatively meager $13,544. Unlike money taken from the other accounts, every dollar withdrawn from the IRA would be taxable. Still, even if taxed in the 50% bracket—leaving $51,987 a year in after-tax income—the IRA owner would be far ahead of those who skipped this tax shelter.

40 YRS./$126,840
35 YRS./$94,836
30 YRS./$69,761
25 YRS./$50,114
20 YRS./$34,719
15 YRS./$22,658
10 YRS./$13,207

Contributions and earnings taxed at 50%

40 YRS./$366,451
35 YRS./$248,731
30 YRS./$166,732
25 YRS./$109,614
20 YRS./$69,829
15 YRS./$42,116
10 YRS./$22,812

Contributions and earnings taxed at 25%

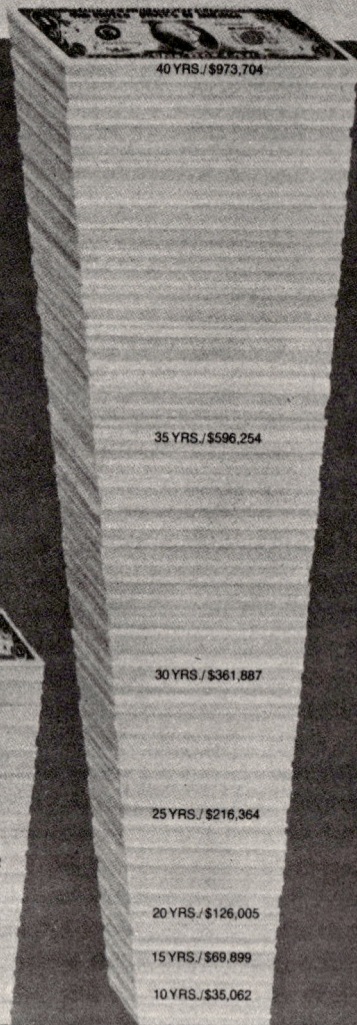

40 YRS./$973,704
35 YRS./$596,254
30 YRS./$361,887
25 YRS./$216,364
20 YRS./$126,005
15 YRS./$69,899
10 YRS./$35,062

Individual Retirement Account

George Shafer

The Plans

As the financial ads in every newspaper demonstrate, there is no shortage of IRA plans to choose from. Your money must be invested through an IRS-approved custodian, which includes commercial banks, savings and loan associations, credit unions, insurance companies, brokerage firms, and mutual fund companies. The endless array of plan options is very confusing to the inexperienced investor.

The most fundamental thing to keep in mind when choosing an IRA plan is that you are making an *investment decision*. Your IRA plan is simply the type of *account* that your investment will be held in. In fact, the short IRA agreement form is the only thing that distinguishes an IRA investment from a non-IRA investment offered by the same financial company. For example, you could invest $4,000 in almost any mutual fund, dividing your money equally between two separate accounts: $2,000 in an IRA account and $2,000 in a non-IRA account. Besides the difference in tax treatment and certain IRA account restrictions, you would have the very same investment with both accounts. An IRA is simply the account, or custodianship, in which you make your investment.

Section III of this book is devoted entirely to the subject of what investments are offered by the various financial companies that act as IRA custodians. The only investments that are not allowed for your IRA money are commodity futures and "collectibles" such as metals, stamps, coins, and artwork. The reason the IRS has recently disallowed collectibles is that it felt people were decorating their own homes with tax-deductible IRA money. There are other investments that are allowable but inappropriate, such as tax shelters (since the IRA account itself is already sheltered).

Claiming Your IRA Tax Deductions

There are no special tax forms to file when you open an IRA or when you fill out your tax return. Just claim your IRA deduction on line 25 of Form 1040 in the section titled "Adjustments to Income."

Form **1040**	Department of the Treasury—Internal Revenue Service **U.S. Individual Income Tax Return** 19**82**		(O)

For the year January 1–December 31, 1982, or other tax year beginning . 1982, ending . 19 . OMB No. 1545-0074

Use IRS label. Otherwise, please print or type.	Your first name and initial (if joint return, also give spouse's name and initial)	Last name	Your social security number
	Present home address (Number and street, including apartment number, or rural route)		Spouse's social security no.
	City, town or post office, State and ZIP code	Your occupation ▶	
		Spouse's occupation ▶	

Presidential Election Campaign ▶ Do you want $1 to go to this fund? . . . Yes / No Note: Checking "Yes" will not increase your tax or reduce your refund.
If joint return, does your spouse want $1 to go to this fund? . . . Yes / No

Filing Status 1 — Single ... filing joint ...

	22	Total income. Add amounts in column for lines 7 through 21 . . . . ▶	22	
Adjustments to Income (See Instructions on page 11)	23	Moving expense (attach Form 3903 or 3903F) . . .	23	
	24	Employee business expenses (attach Form 2106) . .	24	
	25	Payments to an IRA. You must enter code from page 11 (......) . . .	25	
	26	Payments to a Keogh (H.R. 10) retirement plan . . .	26	
	27	Penalty on early withdrawal of savings	27	
	28	Alimony paid	28	
	29	Deduction for a married couple when both work (attach Schedule W)	29	
	30	Disability income exclusion (attach Form 2440) . . .	30	
	31	Total adjustments. Add lines 23 through 30. . . . . ▶	31	
Adjusted Gross Income	32	Adjusted gross income. Subtract line 31 from line 22. If this line is less than $10,000, see "Earned Income Credit" (line 62) on page 15 of Instructions. If you want IRS to figure your tax, see page 3 of Instructions . . . . ▶	32	

How much money does your IRA tax deduction actually save you? It depends on two things: your tax bracket and how much you contribute to your IRA plan.

Most people don't really know what tax bracket they are in. The proposed income tax reductions between 1983 and 1984 don't make these figures any easier to remember. Here is a handy reference table. Remember, the annual incomes in the left column mean *taxable* income, after all deductions have been taken.

Schedule of 1983 and 1984 Tax Rates
Joint Returns

TAXABLE INCOME	1983		1984	
	AMOUNT OF TAX	+ RATE ON EXCESS*	AMOUNT OF TAX	+ RATE ON EXCESS*
0– $3,400	–0–	–0–	–0–	–0–
$3,400– 5,500	–0–	11%	–0–	11%
5,500– 7,600	$231	13	$231	12
7,600– 11,900	504	15	483	14
11,900– 16,000	1,149	17	1,085	16
16,000– 20,200	1,846	19	1,741	18
20,200– 24,600	2,644	23	2,497	22
24,600– 29,900	3,656	26	3,465	25
29,900– 35,200	5,034	30	4,790	28
35,200– 45,800	6,624	35	6,274	33
45,800– 60,000	10,334	40	9,772	38
60,000– 85,600	16,014	44	15,168	42
85,600–109,400	27,278	48	25,920	45
109,400–162,400	38,702	50	36,630	49
162,400–215,400	65,202	50	62,600	50
215,400–	91,702	50	89,100	50

*The amount by which the taxpayer's taxable income exceeds the base of the bracket.

It is a common misconception that one's tax bracket determines the percentage of taxable income that must actually be paid out in federal tax. For the purposes of simplicity, let's look at an example of a high-income figure in the 50 percent tax bracket. Many people think that if a working couple had a combined income of $110,000 after deductions (in 1983), they would have to pay a federal tax bill of $55,000 because they are in the 50 percent bracket (see tax table for Joint Returns—1983). The 50 percent, however, is called the "marginal rate" and only applies to the amount of "excess" income that they earned beyond a certain "base" cutoff figure. In this example, $110,000 of taxable income

Head of Household Returns

TAXABLE INCOME	1983 AMOUNT OF TAX	1983 + RATE ON EXCESS*	1984 AMOUNT OF TAX	1984 + RATE ON EXCESS*
0– $2,300	–0–	–0–	–0–	–0–
$2,300– 4,400	–0–	11%	–0–	11%
4,400– 6,500	$231	13	$231	12
6,500– 8,700	504	15	483	14
8,700– 11,800	834	18	791	17
11,800– 15,000	1,392	19	1,318	18
15,000– 18,200	2,000	21	1,894	20
18,200– 23,500	2,672	25	2,534	24
23,500– 28,800	3,997	29	3,806	28
28,800– 34,100	5,534	34	5,290	32
34,100– 44,700	7,336	37	6,986	35
44,700– 60,600	11,258	44	10,696	42
60,600– 81,800	18,254	48	17,374	45
81,800–108,300	28,430	50	26,914	48
108,300–161,300	41,680	50	39,634	50
161,300–	68,180	50	66,134	50

would be taxed a fixed amount of $38,702 (see table) plus 50 percent of any amount in excess of $109,400 (see table), for a total tax of $39,002 (considerably less than the $55,000 that one might think).

Since an IRA deduction *lowers your excess income,* simply multiply your IRA contributions by your marginal tax bracket to determine your actual savings by taking this deduction. For example, if you make a $2,000 contribution and you are in the 35 percent bracket, then your net savings are $700 in taxes that year.

Changing Your Mind on IRA Investments

If after reading this book you realize you've gotten into the wrong type of IRA plan, don't panic. The IRS

Single Returns

TAXABLE INCOME	1983		1984	
	AMOUNT OF TAX	+ RATE ON EXCESS*	AMOUNT OF TAX	+ RATE ON EXCESS*
0– $2,300	–0–	–0–	–0–	–0–
$2,300– 3,400	–0–	11%	–0–	11%
3,400– 4,400	$121	13	$121	12
4,400– 6,500	251	15	241	14
6,500– 8,500	566	15	535	15
8,500– 10,800	866	17	835	16
10,800– 12,900	1,257	19	1,203	18
12,900– 15,000	1,656	21	1,581	20
15,000– 18,200	2,097	24	2,001	23
18,200– 23,500	2,865	28	2,737	26
23,500– 28,800	4,349	32	4,115	30
28,800– 34,100	6,045	36	5,705	34
34,100– 41,500	7,953	40	7,507	38
41,500– 55,300	10,913	45	10,319	42
55,300– 81,800	17,123	50	16,115	48
81,800–108,300	30,373	50	28,835	50
108,300–	43,623	50	42,085	50

*The amount by which the taxpayer's taxable income exceeds the base of the bracket.

allows you to transfer your plan from one custodian to another as often as you like.

If you decide to switch from a mutual fund IRA to a bank IRA, for example, the bank will be happy to send you a form that authorizes the "direct transfer" of your funds from the mutual fund to the bank. The investments in your old plan are liquidated and your money is sent to the new custodian; you never take possession of the funds yourself in a direct transfer.

You may also take possession of your funds when making an IRA plan transfer, but there are two restrictions in doing so: (1) You must reinvest your funds in a new plan within sixty days. (If you are late, you will be hit with a 10 percent penalty, described below.)

(2) You cannot make this kind of transfer more than once in the same calendar year. In most cases it is simpler and safer to use a direct transfer.

A word of caution: Transferring plans can be expensive. Not only can there be setup fees for your new plan, but there may be withdrawal penalties or termination fees involved in getting out of your old plan. Refer to the table on page 90 for specific fees charged by the various custodians.

Keep in mind that you can change your specific investment without changing the custodianship of your IRA plan. Mutual fund, insurance company, and brokerage plans offer a variety of investment choices for your IRA that can be changed inexpensively as your objectives or the market conditions change.

IRA Rules

THE 10 PERCENT WITHDRAWAL PENALTY

IRAs should be used only for money that you feel absolutely comfortable putting away for retirement. If you have to take money out of your plan before age fifty-nine and a half, for any reason other than a legitimate disability, these are the tax consequences: the amount of your "premature distribution" will be taxed as ordinary income for that year, plus you will have to pay a penalty to the IRS of 10 percent of the amount withdrawn. For example, if you start contributing $2,000 a year to an IRA plan this year and ten years from now, when your plan has grown to $35,000 with contributions and interest, you find that you have to withdraw $10,000 of it for a college tuition, here's what happens: the $10,000 withdrawal will be taxed as ordinary income in that year, plus you will have to pay a $1,000 penalty tax (10 percent of $10,000) that same year. The remaining $25,000 in the IRA plan is not affected.

The custodian of your IRA plan is required to report any premature distribution to the IRS. The taxpayer must use Form 1040 to report the ordinary income and Form 5329 to report the penalty.

Should you start an IRA plan if you just don't know whether you will need to use the money before retirement? This question is no doubt the most difficult consideration for the millions of working Americans who have yet to make their IRA decisions. We should examine the problem closely at this point.

Let's compare the difference between an IRA account and a non-IRA account for the person who must withdraw money, such as in the above example. The exact amount that $2,000 a year contributed for ten years would grow to, using an interest rate of 10 percent, is $35,062. After withdrawing $10,000, you would have to pay as much as $5,000 in taxes (in the 50 percent tax bracket) in addition to the $1,000 penalty. This would leave you with $4,000 from the withdrawal, plus the $25,000 still in your IRA, for a total of *$29,000.*

However, this $29,000 is still more than twice as much as a non-IRA savings account would now be worth, using the same variables ($2,000 a year for 10 years at 10 percent and a 50 percent tax bracket). The non-IRA savings account would now be worth just *$13,207.* Half the contributions and half the interest would have gone to taxes each year.

Ah, but you say that this comparison works only when using the very highest tax brackets. Well, let's see what happens in a 25 percent bracket (about $15,000 individual income in 1983). The same $10,000 IRA withdrawal would lose $2,500 to Uncle Sam in addition to the $1,000 penalty, leaving this person with $6,500 from the withdrawal, plus the $25,000 still in his IRA account, for a total of *$31,500.* This compares very favorably to the value of a non-IRA savings account (using the same variables again) for this 25 percent bracket person too. After ten years his non-IRA savings account would have been worth only $22,812.

Even though taxes would have done less damage to the 25 percent saver than to the 50 percent saver, the message is clear: *The withdrawal penalty is not that great compared to the original tax deductions and other sheltering benefits of having the IRA plan to begin with, in almost any tax bracket.* Even if you are not sure that you can always leave your money in the account, you should probably open an IRA plan. By the time you make that withdrawal, it's even possible that the IRA rules will have been liberalized.

THE 6 PERCENT EXCESS PENALTY

The maximum annual contribution to an IRA plan is $2,000 per working individual. If your spouse does not have earned income, you may contribute an extra $250 from your own income for a special "spousal IRA." The total maximum contribution of $2,250 must be divided into two separate accounts; the contributions can be split in any way as long as neither exceeds $2,000.

There will obviously be many homemakers going on their spouses' payrolls this year for an annual salary of $2,000. What high-income professional couldn't use a part-time bookkeeper for $170 a month? Since there is no longer a percentage-of-income limitation on IRA contributions, a person with total earned income of just $2,000 could contribute the whole thing to an IRA and pay no federal taxes at all. (Most states also accept IRA deductions.)

Don't bother trying to put extra money into your IRA account. Any "overcontributions" in excess of the above limits will not only be disqualified for tax exemption, but will also incur a 6 percent penalty tax. If you contribute $2500 to an individual account, for example, the excess $500 will not be tax deductible and a $30 penalty tax will be levied by the IRS each year until your account is straightened out.

CONTRIBUTION DEADLINES

You don't have to contribute to your IRA plan at the same time as you open your account. In fact, you have until April 15 to make the contribution for the previous tax year. A 1983 contribution, for example, does not have to made until April 15, 1984 (or even later, if you can get an extension on your taxes).

Surely there will be a lot of people waiting until the last minute to make their IRA contributions, but they will be making a big mistake by waiting. The earlier you make your contribution each year, the more time this money will have to grow and the more time it will be protected from taxes. The difference between January contributions and April (a year later) contributions is significant over a long period of time. Consider this example: The difference between investing $4,000 a year at 10 percent for thirty-five years in an IRA on January 1 each year versus April 15 (a year later) each year is *$300,000* at the end of the thirty-five year period. (That's right: the *difference* is $300,000.)

THE 50 PERCENT PENALTY

You cannot make withdrawals from your IRA account before age fifty-nine and a half without incurring a penalty. Between the ages of 59½ and 70½ you can withdraw as little or as much as you want anytime. But starting in the year that you turn seventy and a half, you must withdraw some money each year.

The minimum "distributions" that you must take starting at age seventy and a half are determined by the amount of money that is in your account and by your life expectancy. The reason the IRS requires you to start taking your money out of your IRA plan is because it wants to make sure it gets to tax this money before you die. When you die, whether it's during the contribution or the distribution stage of your IRA, the money in your account goes to your named beneficiary. This person may either take the money and pay tax on it or roll the money into his or her own IRA account, thus prolonging the tax-deferred status.

Below is an actuarial table (ages 70 through 90) for required distributions based on life expectancy information found in the IRS Code:

PRESENT AGE	LIFE EXPECTANCY NO. OF YEARS		PRESENT AGE	LIFE EXPECTANCY NO. OF YEARS	
	MALES	FEMALES		MALES	FEMALES
70	12.1	15.0	81	7.1	9.1
71	11.6	14.4	82	6.7	8.7
72	11.0	13.8	83	6.3	8.3
73	10.5	13.2	84	6.0	7.8
74	10.1	12.6	85	5.7	7.5
75	9.6	12.1	86	5.4	7.1
76	9.1	11.6	87	5.1	6.7
77	8.7	11.0	88	4.8	6.3
78	8.3	10.5	89	4.5	6.0
79	7.8	10.1	90	4.2	5.7
80	7.5	9.6			

In the year that you turn seventy and a half, you must take out at least one twelfth (male) or one fifteenth (female) of your IRA nest egg. The rest of your money can remain in the account; in fact the interest on the remainder should more than replenish that first distribution over the next twelve months.

The next year, at age seventy-one, you must take at least $1/11.6$ (one eleventh) or $1/14.4$ (one fourteenth) out of the account. Again, the remainder could easily replenish your distribution. Most people, however, set up a distribution plan well in excess of the minimums.

What your IRA account is invested in is particularly important when you start taking distributions. While bank instruments and mutual funds are easily divisible, bonds may be more difficult and limited partnerships nearly impossible.

Be very sure you understand the distribution requirements starting at age 70½, because here lies the IRA's stiffest penalty. There is a 50 percent penalty tax on any amount of money that should have been distributed that is not. For example, if your IRA account grows to a value of $1,000,000 by age seventy, your required distribution for the first year would be approximately $80,000. If you forgot to withdraw that amount by the end of that year, you would be hit with a $40,000 tax penalty by the IRS.

While you are taking distributions from your account, remember that the remainding funds in the account continue to grow and remain tax sheltered.

Reaping the Benefits

Much has been said about the wonders of compound interest during the accumulation years of an IRA plan. The media has had no lack of advertisers who illustrate the making of a millionaire simply by socking away a few thousand dollars a year for the rest of your working days.

But surprisingly little has been said about the effects of tax-deferred compounding during the *distribution stage* of an IRA. The effect of this later interest buildup can be considerably more significant than the effect of the earlier compounding because of the much greater sums of money involved. Were it not for the fact that the arithmetic is slightly more complicated to illustrate in an advertisement, I'm sure we would be hearing more about this miracle too.

If the annual tax-deferred contributions can make you a millionaire in twenty-five years while you are working, your accumulated funds can make you a multimillionaire over the next twenty-five years, after you retire, without your contributing another dime. In fact, your funds can do this and still pay you handsome annual distributions in the meantime. The way this works is simple: As you start taking annual distributions during retirement, the remainder of your IRA nest egg continues its tax-deferred buildup. If you have enough in the account by the time you retire, the annual interest coming in can easily exceed the annual distributions going out in the early years of your retirement. The key to this continued compounding, of course, is staying alive. If you die, your plan goes to your beneficiary or your estate.

Here's an impressive scenario: If you retire with an IRA plan worth $500,000 and start taking distributions on a twenty-year actuarial plan, you total *payout* over that period of time could be more than *$2 million* (based on a high interest rate of 12%). When you consider that only about $50,000 may have ever been paid into the plan ($2,000 a year for 25 contributions), it's interesting to see what mathematical tricks the combination of time, tax deferral, and high interest rates can play.

The important thing to remember is that your continuous IRA tax shelter and buildup can be even more significant after you retire than it is while you are working.

6

Special Plans

Payroll Deduction Plans

There are three types of payroll deduction plans your company might offer you this year, and a lot of people seem to be getting them confused.

One plan has been around for a long time and has nothing to do with IRAs: a company thrift or savings plan. I mention it here because it often gets confused with company IRA plans and also because it can be a very attractive alternative to IRAs. Your company may offer to withhold a small percentage of your salary (usually up to 6 percent) from each paycheck and put it in either a savings or an investment plan for you (your choice of plan). Even though there are no tax benefits with this plan, as there are with the IRAs, the big attraction is that your company typically contributes fifty cents for every dollar you put in. Even though you must stay with the plan a minimum number of years in order to collect the company's contributions, your own money is liquid.

The second plan that your employer may offer you this year is an opportunity to invest your IRA money in the company's pension plan (if the company's pension plan has been amended specifically for voluntary employee IRA contributions). The company can make payroll IRA deductions directly into the existing pension plan. You have the same rights and restrictions here that you do in any other IRA plan, plus one small advantage: You don't have to start making withdrawals at age seventy and a half if you don't want to.

The third type of payroll deduction plan will become the most popular this year. This is the program in which your company has signed up an IRA custodian to make its plan available to the company's employees through regular salary deductions. The IRA sponsor (which can be any one of the regular IRA custodian institutions) is solely responsible for the administration of the plan. The only difference between this plan and any individual IRA plan that you might sign up for on your own is that your employer makes the contributions for you directly out of your paycheck. Participation is not a long-term commitment; you can transfer into or out of your company plan whenever you want.

The advantage of payroll deduction plans is convenience. The contributions may be easier to make when they amount to only $38 a week (for the maximum $2,000). The disadvantage of such a plan is that you give up control of the timing of your contributions. The person who contributes a full $2,000 in January, for example, can earn a lot more interest than the person who contributes $38 a week spread out over the entire year. On the other hand, there are a lot of people who will want to wait until the last minute—April 15— before giving up their money. A payroll deduction plan would be of no use for these people.

The main thing to keep in mind when considering a payroll deduction plan is the investment itself. Where will your funds be invested? If your company has chosen a custodian that offers several investment options, be sure that you compare this plan to any other plan you could sign up for on your own. Ask your company's benefit manager the same questions (about the IRA plan that he has chosen) that you would ask your banker or broker about their plans.

IRA Rollovers

Contrary to the way the term is often used, a *rollover* has nothing to do with switching your IRA funds from one custodian to another. That's just called a *transfer* (see page 65).

A rollover is the nontaxable conversion of money from a company pension or profit-sharing account or Keogh account into an IRA plan. This situation is apt to come up when you retire or change jobs.

If you leave your company and are vested in its pension plan, the money that has accrued in your name will be paid out to you. If you do not roll this money into an IRA plan of your own (either an existing plan or a new one) within sixty days, your pension payment automatically becomes taxable in that year. The only part of the distribution that is not taxable would be that portion of the funds that you had contributed to the plan yourself (if your plan had allowed after-tax voluntary contributions). The rest of your distribution is fully taxable if it is not rolled over; although the rate at which it is taxed is favorable (a formula called "ten-year-forward averaging" is used).

Retirees also make extensive use of the IRA rollover provision, and for good reason. Not only will their accumulated pension, profit-sharing, or Keogh funds avoid any current taxation by using the rollover, but that money will be allowed to continue to build up on a tax-deferred basis. There is no limit to the amount of money that can be rolled over from any retirement plan into an IRA.

Whether to roll over your retirement funds or not doesn't have to be an all-or-nothing decision. Since

1978, the IRS has allowed partial rollovers in any proportion that you choose. The only ill effect of splitting this decision is that the amount of money that is distributed (if it's any less than the entirety) is taxed as ordinary income instead of at the favorable ten-year-forward rate. In any rollover, always take out any funds you contributed to the plan voluntarily, since this money is not taxable when it is distributed (because it was taxed before it even went into the pension plan). If you roll your voluntary funds into an IRA, they will be retaxed as ordinary income when your IRA is finally distributed.

If you are covered by a pension or Keogh plan and you change jobs, you can avoid being taxed on the distribution of your retirement funds by rolling this money into an IRA within the sixty-day limit. If your new company's retirement plan will accept rollovers, you can then convert your IRA plan into the new company's plan if you want to.

Once a retirement-plan distribution has been rolled over into an IRA, the same rules and penalties apply to this IRA as to any other IRA plan.

Selecting an IRA Plan

7

Investment Considerations

How Much Money Will You Need When You Retire?

A Rip Van Winkle story can easily be adapted to apply to IRAs and the effect of long-term inflation:

A man falls asleep for forty years and upon awakening immediately calls his banker to check on his IRA. "Congratulations," exclaims the banker, "your IRA is now worth over two million dollars." The man is ecstatic, feeling that his greatest dream has come true. But just then the operator cuts in and says, "One minute is up. Please deposit five hundred dollars."

The first thing you should do when considering any kind of retirement plan is figure out how much income—and therefore how much capital—you will need after you stop working. In the Introduction of this book I mentioned the disappointing fact that a million dollars, thirty-five years from now, is the equivalent of $50,000 today, based on an average inflation rate of 8 percent between now and then.

The table that follows indicates how much more money (how many times the amount) you will need in the future to equal the same amount of money today, depending on the inflation rate.

YEARS UNTIL YOU RETIRE	INFLATION RATE	
	5%	10%
10	1.6	2.6
15	2.0	4.2
20	2.7	6.7
25	3.4	10.8
30	4.3	17.5
35	5.5	28.1

Here's a disturbing example that takes all the fun out of your IRA riches: If you are now forty years old, make $35,000 a year, and would like to have an income when you retire at age sixty-five equivalent to what you have now, look at the table to see how many times your current income you will need then. The table tells us that in twenty-five years you will need almost eleven times what you earn now, given an average inflation rate of 10 percent: approximately $375,000 annual income.

So don't let all those advertisements about getting rich on your IRA fool you. Let's take a close look at what an IRA account will grow to over the years and at what those accumulated funds will actually mean when it comes to producing income in your retirement years. After all, the real purpose of an IRA is to produce income, not to have a huge pot of money to spend.

Here's how money would grow in an IRA account (based on current interest rates and a $2,000 per year contribution), thanks to the wonders of compound interest and the temporary protection from taxes:

YEARS	INTEREST RATE 12%	AMOUNT CONTRIBUTED
5	$ 14,230	$10,000
10	39,309	20,000
15	83,506	30,000
20	161,397	40,000
25	298,667	50,000
30	540,585	60,000
35	966,926	70,000

Even though the IRA tables look impressive, you've got to keep the inflation table in mind. In our earlier example we found that a worker making $35,000 a year at age forty would need an income of $375,000 a year at age sixty-five to maintain the same standard of living, if the cost of living were to increase at an average of 10 percent a year. We now see that if this same person were to invest $2,000 a year in an IRA account for twenty-five years and even achieve an annual yield of 12 percent (consistently beating the inflation rate), the amount would grow to $298,667. This amount of money (even at the same high yield of 12 percent) would produce an income of only about $36,000 a year, compared to the $375,000 that he would need.

There are two things we can learn from comparing the above two tables. The first is that IRAs were never meant to be the sole source of retirement income for anyone. They should be considered just a supplement to other investments, retirement plans, and Social Security. Secondly, it becomes obvious when studying the race between inflation and your money that your most fundamental goal in any investment must be to get a return each year that's at least as high as the inflation rate. Otherwise you are actually losing money.

So your IRA may really make you a millionaire someday; yet being a millionaire probably won't mean much by that time. With this in mind, a good reason to start an IRA plan anyway is so that you won't be the only person around who is not a millionaire during your retirement.

IRA Investment Goals

Can you outperform the cost of living with your investments? If you invest only in the safest, shortest-term and most liquid investments, you will probably only break even. Over the years short-term interest rates have closely paralleled the inflation rate.

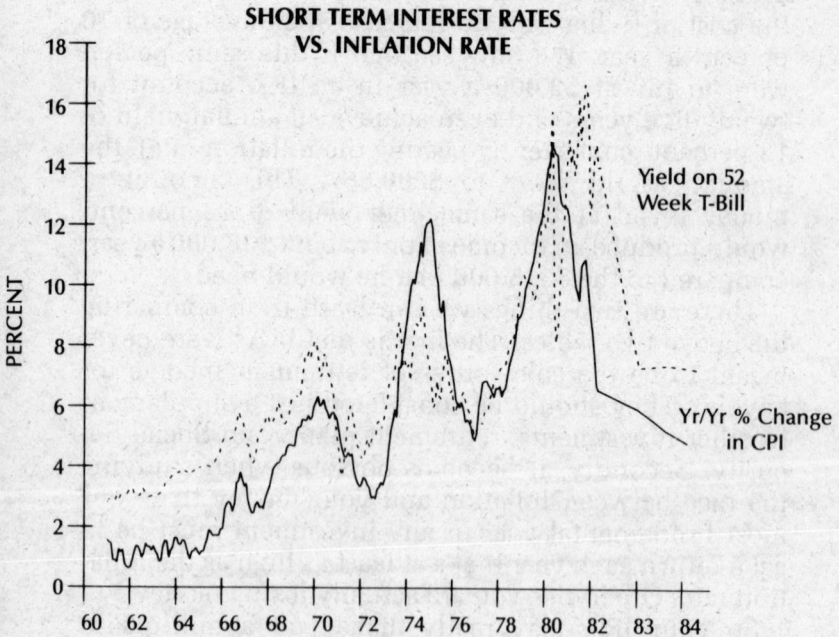

SHORT TERM INTEREST RATES VS. INFLATION RATE

Yield on 52 Week T-Bill

Yr/Yr % Change in CPI

PERCENT

Making a decision about your IRA funds is not much different from making a decision about any other investment. First you define your goals, then you make a judgment about the potential risks and rewards of a variety of investment vehicles.

Besides the special considerations that apply specifically to IRA accounts, such as fees, minimums, penalties, investment flexibility, and convenience (which will all be compared in upcoming chapters), there are four important factors to be considered when making any investment decision:

1. Total investment potential. The most important consideration in any investment is how much money you will have at some point in the future compared to how much you are investing now. If you feel that money market instruments just won't help you achieve your goal of total return, then you will have to try something more aggressive.

2. Risk. Generally speaking, the more return you try to achieve, the most risk you have to take. Money invested in fixed-rate insured bank deposits is at little risk but has little investment potential. Stocks, on the other hand, have high growth potential with relatively high risk.

3. Your overall financial picture. How much risk you should take depends a lot on your current income and future income potential, other investments, and other retirement plans (Keogh, company pension, etc.).

4. Involvement. How involved do you want to be with your investment once you make it? Some people just want to put their money away and forget about it for thirty years. Others get very involved and love trying to outsmart the averages. Savings institutions or even mutual funds would be appropriate vehicles for the less interested, while a self-directed brokerage IRA would be better for those who like to get more involved.

Income vs. Growth for IRAs

Investments can be divided into two basic categories: those whose primary objective is to accumulate income and those whose primary objective is to increase in value.

Income investments are usually *debt instruments*, which means that you are lending money to someone for a certain period of time in return for a certain rate of interest. Your principal, however, may have no chance of increasing in value. Income investments include such instruments as bank deposits, bonds, notes, Treasury bills, and money market funds. High-dividend stocks, such as utilities, are also bought mainly for income.

Growth investments are called *equities* because with them you buy ownership of an asset that you hope will increase in value. Since there is no promise of repayment as there is with debt instruments, the future value of your principal will be determined by what others perceive these assets to be worth at any given time. Stocks and real estate are the two most commonly owned equity investments. While these investments may also produce income, their main investment objective is usually growth in principal value.

Unfortunately there is no agreement among the experts as to which basic investment objective is better for IRA accounts. There are good arguments for each.

The *income advocates*—banks, S & Ls, credit unions, money market funds, and bond funds—have three good arguments.

1. Income investments are generally safer; and this is your retirement money, after all, not your gambling money. Many income investments are insured, and all of them have some kind of repayment promise.

2. Furthermore, investments that pay interest are more predictable. You know exactly how much money you will earn over a given period of time.

3. Thirdly, the income advocates argue, the tax advantages are greater on income IRAs than they are on growth IRAs. Since long-term capital gains tax is now a maximum of only 20 percent and is only charged when the asset is finally sold, protecting growth investments from tax by buying them in an IRA is not a great advantage. Income investments, however, are taxed year by year, and at a rate of up to 50 percent. Here the tax-deferred status does make a significant difference.

So income-oriented IRAs seem to be safer and more predictable and to have better relative tax advantages. They also tend to have lower fees, as you will see in upcoming tables.

But don't stop here and rush out to your nearest savings and loan. The *growth advocates* have some very convincing arguments of their own. The brokerage firms, mutual fund companies, and real estate partnerships (sold through brokerage firms) point out that:

1. Equity ownership is the only chance you have to beat the inflation rate over the years. They point out how the equity markets have always outperformed the debt markets over the longer-term measurements (note the upcoming graphs) and that income investments can at best only keep up with the inflation rate (glance back at the last graph). After all, the growth argument goes, the accumulation of wealth in this country has always been through long-term equity ownership. How many people do you know who have gotten wealthy by lending money? They feel that the risk in good quality growth investments is not that great, and that for most people a $2,000 investment cannot spell financial disaster anyway.

2. Even though the long-term capital gains tax is now only 20 percent maximum, short-term gains (held less than one year) are still taxed up to 50 percent. IRA accounts, therefore, may be the perfect place for some investors to do a little gambling.

3. Another argument for growth-oriented IRAs has to do with today's investment climate. Equities (stocks) still appear to be very underpriced today compared to historical values. (See The Case for Equities, page 126).

In summary: growth-oriented IRAs seem to be our only chance really to build up assets over the years, are probably not that risky with smaller amounts of money, can have certain tax advantages of their own, and may just be at bargain prices right now.

The other factors you should weigh when considering an IRA mostly have to do with your own financial situation and your own opinions about the economy. Your resources and your outlook may certainly change over the years.

The list that follows may be of interest to you now. It shows where the old IRA funds (pre-1982) were invested. Of the approximately $21 billion that was invested in IRA accounts between 1975 and 1982, here's where it went:

savings and loans	$9.4 billion
commercial banks	$4.1 billion
life insurance companies	$3.3 billion
mutual savings banks	$3.3 billion
mutual funds	$1.1 billion

The near absence of mutual funds and brokerage firms, however, was mostly by choice. With the 1982 IRA revisions and explosive popularity, both of these financial institutions are expected to be very competitive. Most experts feel that $21 billion will quickly become the yearly contribution figure instead of the total IRA figure.

How Various Investments Have Performed

A lot of people ask me which investments have performed the best over the longer-term measurements. It is difficult to compare unrelated investments because the objectives of each are different. But the IRA investor should be aware of what the long-term performances have been so that he will be less influenced by recent conditions.

Johnson's Charts, Inc. publishes very helpful financial data that can shed some light on this question. The graphs below show a twenty-year and fifty-six-year record of four different investment vehicles compared to the inflation rate (Consumer Price Index).

Corporate bonds and *U.S. Government (Treasury) bonds* are the most closely related of the four instruments. Both are purchased for the objective of long-term income. (See the section on bonds under Investments for Self-Directed Plans, Chapter 9.) Since corporate bonds are not backed by the government, they pay higher yields than do Treasury bonds. *Commercial paper* represents safe and liquid money for the most conservative investor. Similar vehicles today would be short-term Treasury bills, short-term bank CDs, and money market funds. (See how your money market fund would have performed over the last 50 years.) *Stocks*, of course, are bought for long-term growth by most people.

What's Being Offered for IRAs

The next table compares the general characteristics of the four major IRA custodian types: the savings plans (sponsored by depository institutions such as banks, S & Ls, and credit unions), the self-directed plans (sponsored by brokers), the mutual fund plans, and the insurance company plans.

Before going into greater detail about each of these custodian categories, comparing their common fea-

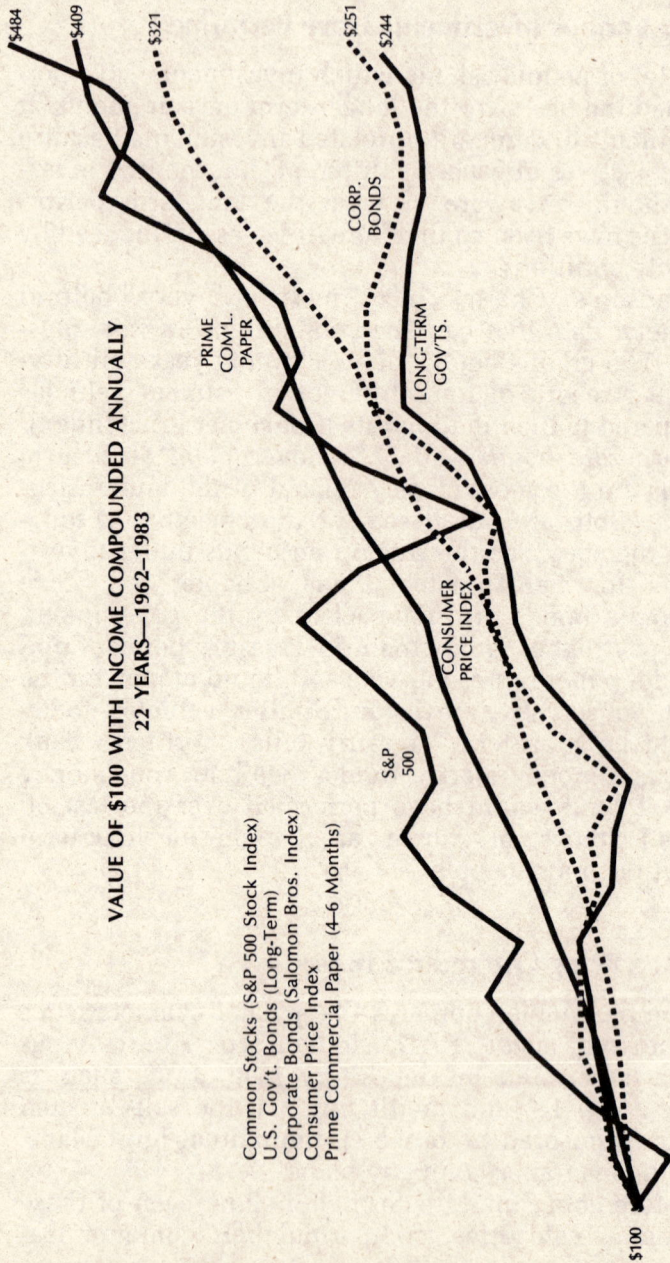

VALUE OF $100 WITH INCOME COMPOUNDED ANNUALLY
22 YEARS—1962–1983

Common Stocks (S&P 500 Stock Index)
U.S. Gov't. Bonds (Long-Term)
Corporate Bonds (Salomon Bros. Index)
Consumer Price Index
Prime Commercial Paper (4–6 Months)

PRIME
COM'L.
PAPER

CORP.
BONDS

LONG-TERM
GOVTS.

CONSUMER
PRICE INDEX

S&P
500

$484
$409
$321
$251
$244

$100

1962 1963 1964 1965 1966 1967 1968 1969 1970 1971 1972 1973 1974 1975 1976 1977 1978 1979 1980 1981 1982 1983

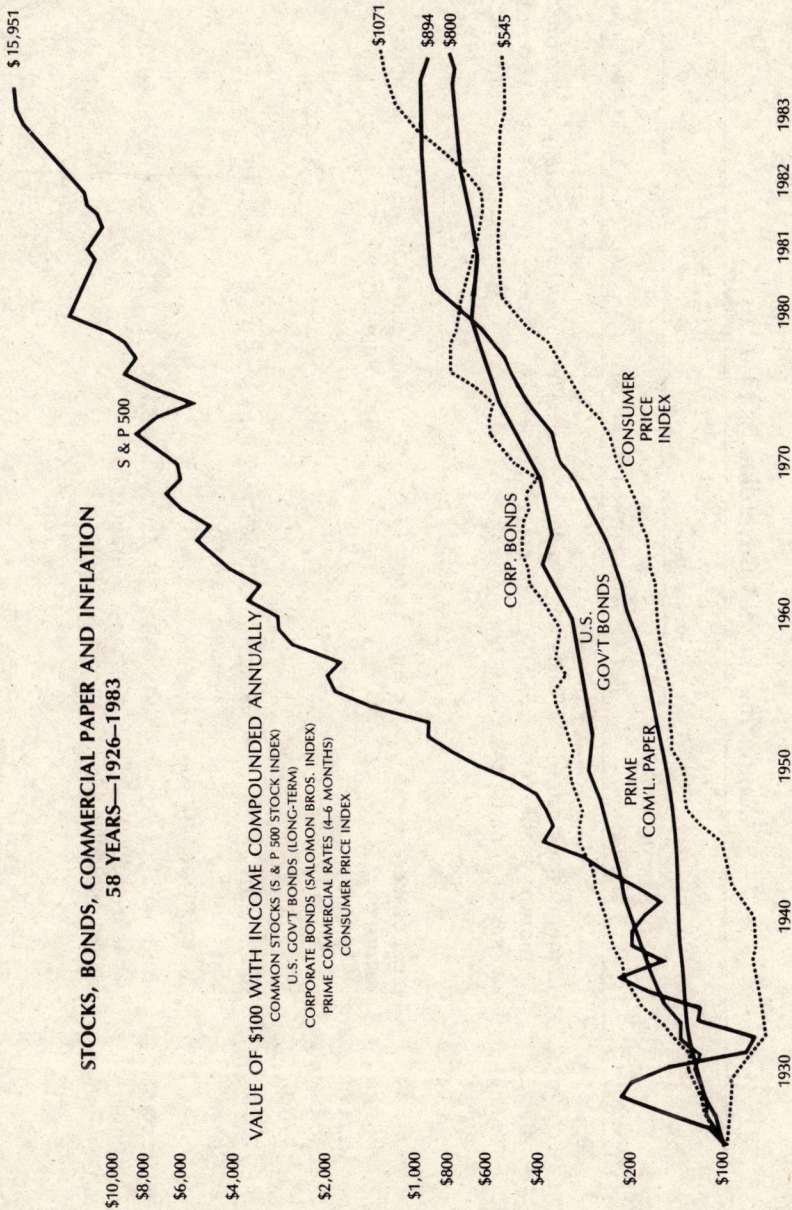

STOCKS, BONDS, COMMERCIAL PAPER AND INFLATION
58 YEARS—1926—1983

VALUE OF $100 WITH INCOME COMPOUNDED ANNUALLY

COMMON STOCKS (S & P 500 STOCK INDEX)
U.S. GOV'T BONDS (LONG-TERM)
CORPORATE BONDS (SALOMON BROS. INDEX)
PRIME COMMERCIAL RATES (4—6 MONTHS)
CONSUMER PRICE INDEX

S & P 500

$15,951

$10,000
$8,000
$6,000
$4,000

$2,000

$1,000
$800
$600

$400

$200

$100

$1071
$894
$800

$545

CORP. BONDS

U.S.
GOV'T BONDS

PRIME
COM'L. PAPER

CONSUMER
PRICE
INDEX

1930   1940   1950   1960   1970   1980   1981   1982   1983

Comparing the IRA Custodian Institutions

CUSTODIAN	INVESTMENT CHOICES	USUAL MINIMUMS		FEES			
		INITIAL	ADDITIONAL	INITIAL	ANNUAL	TRANSFER	WITHDRAWAL
Depository Accounts (Banks, credit unions, S & Ls)	18-month fixed rate 18-month variable rate several other maturities	$250–$500 average	usually none	usually none	usually none	usually none	3 month– 12 month interest
Self-Directed Accounts (brokerage firms)	most brokerage securities	none	none	$20–$30 plus commissions	$20–$150	none	none
Mutual Funds	stock funds bond funds money market funds	$500 average	$50–$250 average	0–8½%	0–$15	0–$10	none
Insurance Annuities	Fixed-rate (bonds) variable (stocks) money market funds	$15–$50 average	$15–$50 average	0–8¾%	0–$30	none	0–10%

tures can be very helpful. What do you get when you go
to a broker to open an IRA account, compared to what
you get at your bank? What are the fees involved with
the mutual fund plans as compared to the insurance
plans? Which type of plan has the least risk; the highest
interest rate; the greatest growth potential?

The person who finally chooses a self-directed plan
is making a completely different investment decision
from the person who ends up choosing a savings plan.
The purpose of the following table—and of the next
five chapters—is to help you make a knowledgeable
decision about which specific IRA plan is best for you.

8

Savings Plans

The depository institutions—banks, S & Ls, and credit unions—offer the simplest, safest, and least expensive way to own an IRA.

You can invest your IRA money in any traditional form of insured deposit that will accept as little as $2,000. The only savings investments that cannot be used for IRA are the $10,000 six-month CD (certificate of deposit) and the uninsured repurchase agreements.

Wild Cards

The savings institutions' toughest competitor for your retirement dollars, however, is a new type of certificate, designed and approved for IRA, called the *wild-card* CD. Unlike every other kind of bank certificate in 1982, these new CDs had no ceilings imposed on their interest rates. Each bank and S & L sets its own competitive rate. The new certificate must be at least eighteen months in term and may be longer.

Wild cards come in two styles: fixed-rate and variable-rate. The *fixed-rate* yields are determined by some standard measurement chosen by the bank, such as Treasury bill rates or the bank's current cost of borrowing money. What a bank offers as its fixed rate will change during the year, but once you lock in a particular rate for your IRA, then that rate is set for the full eighteen months. The current rates that most banks and S & Ls offered in mid-1983 were in the 8 to 10 percent range. Taking the time to make a few phone calls to compare rates is obviously worth it.

With the eighteen-month *variable-rate* certificate, the interest rate on your money will change periodically between the time you purchase it and the time it matures; the most common intervals for rate adjustments are weekly and monthly. Some banks guarantee a minimum interest rate. Citibank, for example, guaranteed a minimum of 10 percent on its variable-rate CD, with no maximum rate, when first offered in 1982.

Whether you choose the fixed-rate certificate or the variable-rate certificate depends on what you think interest rates are going to do over the next eighteen months. A 10 percent fixed rate may look attractive at first but then seem very low if interest rates soared back up to 14 percent after you locked in the lower rate. The variable-rate investment was designed to be competitive with the popular money market funds offered by other financial institutions, which adjust their rates every day.

The current rates offered by most banks and S & Ls on variable-rate CDs in mid-1983 ranged from 8 percent to about 10 percent. Here is what a few of the banks and S & Ls in the Washington, D.C., area were offering at that time for both fixed- and variable-rate eighteen-month CDs for IRAs:

BANKS	18-MONTH FIXED RATE	18-MONTH VARIABLE RATE
American Security	9.50%	8.66%
Riggs National	9.50%	8.72%
First American	—	9.23%
S & Ls		
Columbia First Federal	10.35%	10.35%
Metropolitan Federal	9.8%	9.3%

When a CD of any maturity comes due, whether in an IRA or non-IRA account, another decision must be made about how to reinvest the funds. Typically, you would receive a note from your bank about two weeks before maturity, reminding you that funds are coming due and that they will be reinvested in the same instrument unless the bank is instructed otherwise. Your choices at this time, of course, include using a CD different in type or maturity, or even switching your entire account from that bank to another custodianship.

Compounding

How the interest is compounded is very important when comparing IRA plans offered by the savings institutions. Be sure you know whether your interest gets compounded daily, weekly, monthly, quarterly, or annually. The common denominator in compound interest is called the *effective annual yield,* which tells you the total effect of any compounding for the whole year. Consider this calculation: $2,000 invested in an IRA each year for thirty years, compounded *annually* at 10 percent builds up to about $360,000. The same amount of money, invested for the same length of time at the same rate but compounded *daily,* will build up to about $460,000.

Be sure that you understand not only how your bank compounds its interest but how it figures length to maturity on your IRA contributions. Some banks, for example, require the full eighteen-month holding period on each deposit, while others allow additional deposits into the original eighteen-month time period. This can be important if you expect to make regular deposits into the plan.

Penalties for Early Withdrawal

Perhaps the biggest drawback of using the savings institutions for IRAs is the mandatory penalty for early withdrawal. The government requires banks and S & Ls to withhold a minimum of three months' interest against certificates maturing in one year or less, and at least six months' interest against certificates of more than a year if either is withdrawn before maturity. (These penalties are in addition to the IRS-imposed penalty of 10 percent for taking money out of the IRA plan itself.) The only exception to this rule is if the IRA certificate owner is age 59½ or older. Even then the custodian may impose the penalty if it chooses.

The withdrawal penalties may be a problem for people who are apt to change their goals as the economy and investment climates change. Only the IRA funds that have already been deposited, however, are committed to that particular time period. New money going into an IRA each year can be directed to other investments if your objectives change. Also keep in mind that an eighteen-month maturity is really a very short-term commitment, so the withdrawal penalties should not be much of a problem.

Fees and Insurance

The safety and inexpensiveness of a depository-institution IRA are unquestionable. All federally chartered institutions are insured for $100,000 per account by the FDIC (for banks), the FSLIC (for S & Ls), or the National Credit Union Administration. This insurance is backed by the full faith and credit of the federal government. Most of the depository-institution IRA plans charge no fees at all for either opening an account or for maintaining it, but some plans charge a nominal fee of about $10 a year. Be sure you know whether your IRA account is federally insured and if there are any fees connected to the plan.

Competition for Your IRA

The competition for IRA accounts is probably fiercest among the banking and savings institutions. Since the depository institutions have been the custodians for the vast majority of IRA funds in the past (75 percent of the pre-1982 accounts), they are determined to get their share of the billions of new dollars rolling into this year's IRAs. The insurance, mutual fund, and brokerage custodians, however, are now in the thick of the competition for these same IRA accounts that they previously considered too small to fight over.

This year's barrage of advertising, extolling the virtues of compound interest and tax deductions, is bewildering. Because of their recent hardships, the savings institutions are going the furthest in the use of gimmicks and bonuses to attract new funds. Consider some of the efforts used in 1982 during the early stages of IRA competition:

1. The American Bankers Association spent $3 million dollars for magazine and television ads to promote bank IRAs.

2. Merchants National Bank of Cedar Rapids, Iowa, offered a *50 percent interest* rate (for three months) on new IRA deposits, until they got so many accounts that they had to discontinue the promotion.

3. Bank of America, the nation's largest bank, offered its IRA customers participation in a drawing for prizes ranging from TV sets to vacation cruises to a grand prize of $50,000.

How much the nation's economy or the savings industry will ultimately benefit from the new IRAs is yet to be determined. The intense competition for accounts has certainly increased the costs of IRA accounts for the financial companies, with each one trying to pay a slightly higher interest rate than the others. Also, the depository custodians report, much of the IRA funds they are receiving is not new money. About 65 percent of their IRA deposits come from other savings accounts, mostly within the same institution.

Checklist Before Signing Up

There is not a lot of risk in using a depository IRA.

But, as with any investment in any type of account, there are certain things that you should be sure you understand before signing up. Here is a checklist for bank, S & L, and credit-union IRAs:

1. Call around for the latest *interest rates*. As demonstrated earlier in this chapter, there can be a significant difference between rates at two institutions offering the exact same certificate.

2. See if there are any *fees* of any kind associated with an institution's IRA plans.

3. How is the interest *compounded*—daily, weekly, monthly, or annually? Ask for the effective annual yield.

4. For variable-rate certificates, find out how often the rate adjustments are made and what they are based on.

5. Ask if the nonmandatory withdrawal penalty for people over 59½ is charged, even if you are much younger than that yourself.

6. Be sure you understand how additional deposits are figured in regard to maturity dates and early withdrawal penalties.

7. Be sure, of course, that the institution you are considering is insured by the FDIC, FSLIC, or National Credit Union Administration.

Who Should Use a Savings IRA?

Depository IRAs are probably the best plan for most inexperienced investors. The advantages of complete safety, simplicity, and absence of fees are very significant. The current interest rates and premium competition among these institutions for your account only add to their appeal as a group. And the fact that you will be adding much needed capital to your own community and to the suffering national economy through your local savings institution is even added incentive.

Lack of principal growth and investment flexibility don't matter to most people, because they don't want to take the risk that's always inherent with growth potential. The withdrawal penalties should seldom pose a problem with maturities as short as eighteen months; most people can foresee the need for liquidity within that period of time. The sudden withdrawal loss potential is actually much greater with most other IRA plans, because they could be sold at a principal loss due to market fluctuations.

ADVANTAGES OF BANK AND S & L IRAs

Even though there are several ways to compound interest, most of the commercial banks compound daily. Some of the other custodians are not as generous.

A commercial bank may be the most convenient place for you to have your IRA account, particularly if you are already using the bank for other financial services. You may feel more confident starting this new account with someone you already know and trust.

Most banks allow very low minimum IRA deposits and incremental contributions and offer automatic transfer of funds from your checking or savings account to your IRA once it is set up; they are well equipped to handle the small depositor, who, until recently, was largely ignored by many of the other institutions. The banks encourage IRA accounts of any size, welcoming the $500- and $1000-a-year person as much as the $2,000 and $2,250 IRA depositor. The following table illustrates the significance of these smaller deposits over a long period of time.

Despite the much publicized financial troubles of the S & Ls in 1981 and 1982, it must be emphasized that there is absolutely no risk in S & L deposits, since they are fully insured by the federal government. The S & Ls continue, at this writing, to be the leaders in IRA business.

The two principal reasons that the S & Ls have been

Sample Individual Retirement Account Chart

Interest Rate: 12% *Compounded Annually.*
Figures Are Rounded to the Nearest Dollar.

YEAR	$500 ($9.62/Week)	$1,000 ($19.23/Week)	$1,500 ($28.85/Week)	$2,000 ($38.46/Week)	$2,250 ($43.27/Week)
1	$ 560	$ 1,120	$ 1,680	$ 2,240	$ 2,520
2	1,187	2,374	3,562	3,749	5,342
3	1,890	3,799	5,669	7,559	8,503
4	2,676	5,353	8,029	10,706	12,044
5	3,558	7,115	10,673	14,230	16,009
6	4,545	9,089	13,634	18,178	20,450
7	5,650	11,300	16,950	22,599	25,424
8	6,888	13,776	20,663	27,551	30,995
9	8,274	16,549	24,823	33,097	37,235
10	9,827	19,655	29,482	39,309	44,223
11	11,567	23,133	34,699	46,266	52,050
12	13,515	27,029	40,544	54,058	60,816
13	15,696	31,393	47,089	62,785	70,633
14	18,140	36,280	54,420	72,559	81,629
15	20,877	41,753	62,630	83,507	93,945
16	23,942	47,884	71,826	95,767	107,738
17	27,375	54,750	82,125	109,499	123,187
18	31,220	62,440	93,660	124,879	140,489
19	35,526	71,052	106,579	142,105	159,868
20	40,349	80,699	121,048	161,397	181,572
21	45,751	91,503	137,254	183,005	205,881
22	51,801	103,603	155,404	207,206	233,107
23	58,578	117,155	175,733	234,310	263,599
24	66,167	132,334	198,501	264,668	297,751
25	74,667	149,334	224,001	298,668	336,001
26	84,187	168,374	252,561	336,748	378,842
27	94,849	189,699	284,548	379,398	426,823
28	106,791	213,583	320,374	427,166	480,561
29	120,166	240,333	360,499	480,665	540,749
30	135,146	270,293	405,439	540,585	608,158
31	151,924	303,848	455,772	607,695	683,657
32	170,715	341,429	512,144	682,859	768,216
33	191,760	383,521	575,281	767,042	862,922
34	215,332	430,664	645,995	861,327	968,993
35	241,732	483,463	725,195	966,926	1,087,792
36	271,299	542,599	813,898	1,085,197	1,220,847
37	304,415	608,831	913,246	1,217,661	1,369,869
38	341,505	683,010	1,024,515	1,366,020	1,536,773
39	383,046	766,091	1,149,137	1,532,183	1,723,706
40	429,571	859,142	1,288,714	1,718,285	1,933,070

Source: American Bankers Association. Based on the current approximate yield of 12% for 30-month certificates of deposit. This rate is not intended to be a statement of the actual interest rate available or guaranteed end financial results.

the IRA leaders since 1975 are because they went after the small investor and because the S & Ls were, until recently, allowed to pay a slightly higher interest rate than the commercial banks.

Since S & Ls are the primary source of home mortgages, an IRA account with this institution can help home buyers in the local housing market by helping enlarge the total supply of mortgage money available.

In summary, the IRA plans being offered by banks, S & Ls, and credit unions are ideal for people who cannot afford to lose any money. This would include people who just don't have the risk-taking temperament for other investments as well as people who are limited in income, other retirement resources, or total liquid reserves. I would also recommend the depository IRAs for the majority of first-time investors and for investors close to retirement age.

Choosing a Bank or S & L for Your IRA

There are two considerations that you should weigh when deciding on which particular depository institution to use for you IRA account, if you feel that this type of custodianship plan is best for you.

The first consideration is simply an objective comparison of the interest rates offered by each bank and S & L in your area. Many newspapers around the country have conducted surveys and printed lists of rates offered by institutions in their cities. If you don't find such a survey or if you need more updated information, just get out your Yellow Pages and make some calls yourself. It's worth the time.

The other consideration has to do with your overall banking needs. Every investor needs a "financial team," which should consist of the following specialists: accountant or tax adviser; attorney; broker or investment adviser; and banker. Each of these people has a separate field of expertise. Your lawyer, for example, doesn't necessarily know a thing about investments.

And your broker may not know anything about taxes.

A lot of people underestimate their need for a good banking relationship. But a banker can be a very helpful member of your financial team. If you don't already have a person whom you can identify as "your banker," then I would recommend using your IRA as an opportunity to start a relationship that could help you in other financial matters. Your bank can help you with any of the following: getting a quick loan in an emergency situation (which is no time to be initiating the lengthy process of establishing credit), financing assistance and advice on a real estate transaction, advice on getting legal or tax assistance, help in planning overseas travel, help in getting cash or credit if you are out of town, safe-deposit boxes, help in estate settlements, retirement planning, and general financial planning. Your banker may also be a valuable business contact for you because of his or her familiarity with other business and professional people in your community.

You may find it convenient to have your checking and savings account at the same bank as your IRA. Introduce yourself to the branch manager of the bank you are considering; he should welcome your business. Tell the manager about your needs and see what kind of services that bank can offer.

If you are new in town, you might want to take a look at Polk's *World Bank Directory*. Available in most libraries, this guide lists thousands of banks with addresses, services offered, and names of officers to contact.

What's Being Offered

The following table compares specific IRA products offered by some of the Washington, D.C. area depository institutions. Represented is a random sampling of three banks, three S & Ls, and three credit unions. The interest rates stated were the ones available at each company in mid-1983.

IRA Characteristics of the Depository Institutions:
(Exactly what's being offered for IRAs by certain banks, S & Ls, and credit unions)

	INVESTMENT CHOICES	INTEREST RATES*	MINIMUM INVESTMENT INITIAL	MINIMUM INVESTMENT INCREMENT	WITHDRAWAL PENALTIES	WHERE YOU CAN GET INFORMATION ON THIS TYPE OF INSTITUTION IN YOUR AREA
BANKS						
American Security	18-month fixed	9.50%	$250	none	6 months interest	American Bankers Association 1120 Connecticut Avenue Washington, D.C. 20036 (202) 467-4000
	18-month variable	8.66%				
National Savings Trust	18-month fixed	8.05%	$100	none	same	
	18-month variable	8.05%				
Riggs National	18-month fixed	9.50%	$500	$50	same	
	18-month variable	8.72%				
S & Ls						
Columbia 1st Federal	18-month fixed	10.35%	none	none	6 months interest	U.S. League of Savings Associations 111 East Wacker Drive Chicago, IL 60601 (312) 644-3100
	18-month variable	10.35%				
First Maryland	19-month fixed	10.50%	$500	$100	same	
	19-month variable	9.72%				

						Credit Union National Association 1730 Rhode Island Ave., N.W. Washington, D.C. 20036 (202) 659-2360
Interstate Federal	30-month fixed / 18-month variable	9.95% / 10.45%	$100	none	same	
CREDIT UNIONS						
Agriculture Federal Credit Union	share account	10%	none	none	3 months interest	
Navy Federal Credit Union	share account	11.45%	none	none	none	
State Department Federal Credit Union	share account	10.5%	none	none	none	

*As of May 1983.

9

Self-Directed Brokerage Plans

The self-directed IRA plans offer the greatest variety of investment selection, yet cost the most to open and maintain.

A self-directed IRA is simply a brokerage account with a few IRA restrictions. When you open a self-directed IRA account, you get whatever services generally come with having any kind of account at the same brokerage house. These services will include research information on securities, other investment help for your non-IRA money, and a broker who will be assigned to your account. Your IRA account is different from a regular brokerage account only in the following ways: (1) You are not allowed to buy commodity futures or collectibles in your IRA account. (2) You are limited to adding only $2,000 of new money per year to your account. (3) You cannot take money out of the account without incurring the IRS penalty (except to transfer it to another IRA account.) (4) You cannot put your IRA account on margin (borrow money against your securities).

Advantages and Disadvantages

The key to self-directed plans is flexibility. In the world of ever-changing investment opportunities, flexibility can be a great advantage to someone with the interest and knowledge to benefit from market trends. The ability to switch quickly out of a money market fund into stocks or bonds when interest rates begin to fall, for example, can certainly be more profitable than having money tied up in a fixed annuity or certificate of deposit.

Self-directed plans also offer a greater variety of investments than the other custodianships. Besides stocks and bonds, the brokerage IRAs generally offer money market funds, government securities, CDs, annuities, their own mutual funds, options, real estate partnerships, and unit trusts.

Experienced investors often prefer self-directed IRA plans because they have control over the account. They can keep their funds in the same safe vehicles that the depository institutions offer (CDs, money market funds) yet switch to something else whenever they want.

Some people see a self-directed IRA plan as a place to speculate a little. Their argument is that an IRA plan is a good place to take short-term capital gains, since all the tax within this account is deferred until retirement. Normally, investment profits taken in less than one year are fully taxed at a rate equal to that of your earned income. A self-directed IRA may be an ideal place for more active trading of securities without the worry of losing half your profits to Uncle Sam. The built-in safety net of such an account is the limitation of funds that you are allowed to add to the account each year.

Another argument for self-directed plans has to do with profit potential. The brokers' plans do offer at least the possibility for unlimited growth. After all, there really are people who have made fortunes in the stock market starting with relatively little. No one has ever gotten rich, however, by investing in mutual funds, annuities, or savings plans.

While the self-directed plans are the most flexible and the most diverse in investment choice and do offer the sophisticated investor more control, more profit potential, and some otherwise unavailable tax incentives, they are certainly not for everyone.

The most obvious disadvantage of the self-directed plans is the cost. Most brokerage houses charge an initial setup fee as well as an annual management fee. One major firm charges $30 initially and $50 per year, which combine to take a 4 percent bite out of your first year's $2,000. Keep in mind, however, that the setup fee is charged only once and that the annual charge (if it's a fixed fee) will shrink as a percentage of your assets each year as you contribute more money to your account.

Here is what some brokers are charging for IRA accounts in 1983. You will also incur the broker's standard commission fees for each transaction you make once the account is open. The average cost of a $2,000 stock transaction (buying or selling) is about 2½ percent. Larger transactions cost less, of course. Some brokerage firms also charge termination fees for closing out an IRA account.

	INITIAL FEE	MINIMUM ANNUAL FEE
Dean Witter Reynolds	$20	$20
Bache Halsey Stuart	25	50
Shearson/American Express	None	50
E. F. Hutton	None	25
Kidder Peabody	25	25
Legg Mason	25	25
Paine Webber	25	25
Alex Brown	25	35

All these fees should be weighed against your potential profits and the extra fulfillment you may achieve by handling your own plan.

The next obvious disadvantage of the self-directed approach is the risk factor. There's no question that you take more risk trading stocks on your own, for example, than you do by sticking your money in a high-quality mutual fund, an insurance annuity, or a savings plan. How many people do you know who have made money in the stock market over the last ten years? Yet millions of people continue to try to outsmart the odds every year.

While investment variety is the trademark of the brokers' plans, the limitation on IRA funds is more of a problem with these plans that it is with any of the others. It is difficult to invest only $2,000 or $4,000 in the stock market; the lack of diversification only adds to your risk.

If the confident self-directed advocates recommend using your IRA account for trading to avoid short-term capital gains tax, what happens if there are no gains? The other side of the tax coin in IRAs is the fact that *losses* (short- or long-term) are not tax deductible if they occur in an IRA account. Capital losses are normaly deductible against either gains or income, which helps cushion some of the blow of a bad investment. In an IRA, however, losses have no tax benefit at all.

Another tax consideration of IRAs has to do with long-term capital gains. Normally only 40 percent of a long-term gain is taxable, which means that the maximum tax paid on such gains is only 20 percent (40 percent taxable × 50 percent bracket). In an IRA account, however, the eventual distribution of all your accumulated funds (whether they came from interest, dividends, or capital gains) will be fully taxed as *income*. This means that the tax rate could be as high as 50 percent, even on money that resulted from long-term capital gains that would have otherwise been taxed at only 20 percent.

The tax ramifications of IRA plans are these: short-term gains are deferred and eventually taxed at the same rate; long-term gains are deferred but eventually taxed at a higher rate; and all losses have no tax consequence at all.

In summary, the brokerge IRA plans do have more diverse products available and more potential for profit, allow you more control, and have certain tax advantages over any of the other plans. On the other hand, these self-directed plans are the most expensive and riskiest IRAs and have certain tax disadvantages.

Who Should Use a Self-Directed Plan?

The brokerage IRAs are the very best plan for some people and the very worst plan for others. The majority of first-time IRA investors do not need a self-directed plan simply because they don't have enough IRA money yet to buy most securities.

The first criterion I use in determining suitability for self-directed plans is the amount of money available. Unless you have in the neighborhood of $10,000 already in your IRA plan, you should choose one of the other plans at least initially. This means that the brokerage IRAs are mainly for people who were eligible for IRA plans prior to 1982 and have been accumulating funds over the years. It's not unusual to find an IRA account already worth $15,000 that was started when the old IRA came into being in 1975. If you do have an existing IRA account under any custodianship and want the advantages of a self-directed account, transferring the account to a broker is easy to do.

The other way you may have even more sizable funds already available for IRA is through a *rollover* from a Keogh, pension plan, or profit-sharing account (a rollover simply being the conversion of funds out of another type of retirement plan into an IRA without incurring any taxes; see page 75).

If you don't already have $10,000 in your IRA plan,

you ought to wait a few years until you do before using a self-directed plan. A depository plan, for example, will grow to $10,000 in just four years of $2,000 deposits plus interest.

Besides having enough money, a self-directed investor must have the right temperament, knowledge, and interest for making investment decisions. To invest in securities, particularly stocks, you have to enjoy spending some time keeping abreast of the financial markets.

Since the self-directed investor is usually looking for growth and is taking some risk to get growth, it helps to be relatively young and to have an adequate income. I would not recommend the brokers' IRAs for older people or for people with no other retirement plan. People with good company or government pension plans or plenty of reserve assets who are using an IRA mainly as a tax deduction may be more inclined to go with a self-directed plan with only $2,000 initially. Also, a younger person may want to use an IRA plan as an introduction to the financial markets and to establish a working relationship with a stockbroker who may be able to help with other money services over the years.

Your IRA Brokerage Account

Your investment broker should be an important member of your financial team. The best way to find a good broker is the same way you find a good doctor, lawyer, or plumber: Ask people whose opinion you respect. If your banker recommends a stockbroker to you, chances are you'll get better service than you would by just walking into a brokerage office and asking to be assigned to a broker. Brokers value referral business from their existing clients dearly.

It is generally recommended that you choose a full-service brokerage firm that is a member of the New York Stock Exchange. Full-service firms do a lot more than just execute transactions. They provide you with a variety of other financial services (see the discussion of Financial Supermarkets beginning on page 35) as well as timely research reports on securities you are interested in and help from a professional who should be familiar with most of the money concerns you have today.

The New York Stock Exchange (NYSE) has about five-hundred member firms, which do about 90 percent of all the securities business in the United States. The NYSE standards are easily the strictest in the industry and include the maintenance of certain capital requirements as well as surprise audits by both the exchange and its independent CPA firms.

Brokers who work for NYSE firms are also governed by the strictest rules and ethical standards in the industry. Just to be licensed, they must take a specific training course and pass the NYSE's own licensing examination. Although these basic suggestions won't guarantee a good broker relationship and certainly won't promise success in the market, a full-service NYSE firm is more likely to provide you with the investment help you will need over a long period of time.

Convenience is another important factor in choosing your broker for an IRA account. Although the majority of securities transactions are made over the phone, it helps to stop in to see your broker from time to time so that he or she will become more familiar with your changing needs and more apt to look out for you as a friend as well as a customer.

Opening an IRA brokerage account—or a regular brokerage account—is as easy as starting a checking account at a bank. The broker will ask for your address, phone number, Social Security number, bank reference, what kind of work you do, and a general picture of your financial situation. The more detail you can give about your income, other investments and assets, retirement funds, tax situation, and financial goals, the more the broker will be able to help you in areas beyond your IRA account.

Your broker's job is to help you make good investment decisions. Consider his advice and judgment, and read the brokerage company's research reports; but every decision is ultimately your own. If you use a self-directed plan, you must get involved with the account yourself. Try to develop a good working relationship with your broker, but don't expect perfection in the recommendations you get. Few brokers are financially independent. How right should a broker be? With stocks, if you are right more often than wrong, you'll make money.

Investments for Self-Directed Plans

Since your IRA decision is really an investment decision and opening a self-directed plan is really the same as opening any small brokerage account, an examination of the specific investment vehicles used in the brokerage plans is necessary. What are the risks and opportunities of each of these specific investments, compared to using the more passive investments offered by the other custodian plans?

STOCKS FOR IRAs
The best reason to invest in stocks with your IRA money is a belief that stocks, in general, will outperform other investments in the long run. It is true that stocks have beaten bonds and savings in the past. Between the mid-1920s and mid-1970s, for example, the average NYSE stock would have turned $2,000 into about $140,000, for a 9 percent average annual return. The same amount of money invested in corporate bonds during that time would be worth only about $13,000, for an annual return of less than 4 percent.

The return on Treasury bills and savings accounts would have been even lower than the bonds, of course. (Keep in mind that the average inflation rate during this entire period was only 2.3 percent.) Take a close look at the graph on page 89, which compares the performance of stocks to various other investments since 1926.

To be a long-term investor in stocks, you must believe in long-term economic growth. But many people now question America's future productivity. Inflation has been a devastating problem in recent years, and a deep recession has been gripping this nation. Industry today faces enormous problems of government regulation, labor union demands, and scarcity of natural resources.

If you do believe in continued productivity and you do like the idea of owning part of a corporation, how do you figure out what a particular stock is really worth? The only true answer to this question is that a stock is worth whatever someone is willing to pay for it. The two most common measurements of value in stocks, however, have to do with various perceptions of their *earnings* and of their *assets*. It's helpful to be familiar with a few of the terms that are commonly used in reference to determining stock values.

Earnings per share is a term used to indicate a company's total net after-tax earnings (profits) for one year, divided by the total number of shares that make up the ownership of the company. If a company has total sales of its products or services totaling $100 million for a year, and its total expenses and taxes amount to $90 million, then its net earnings would be $10 million. If the company has 5 million shares outstanding, then its earnings per share would amount to $2. The company would have $2 of net earnings representing every share of its stock.

Price-earning ratio is the current price of a stock divided by its earnings per share. So if our company that has earnings of $2 per share were trading on the stock market for $18, we would say that it has a PE ration of 9 (or 9 : 1).

PE ratios are commonly used to measure the relative value of a stock. Generally speaking, the lower the PE is, the better value the stock price is. But of course there are reasons that some stocks sell at higher "multiples" than others. More highly regarded stocks (or stocks that are generally expected to be increasing their earnings in upcoming years) may be trading at much higher multiples than stocks whose earnings are expected to drop. The average PE ratio on the New York Stock Exchange in mid-1982 was about 7 : 1, which was historically very low. A year later, after one of the greatest stock market rallies in history, the NYSE price-earnings ratio stood at about 13 : 1. The range on all stocks, however, is very wide: from low PEs of 5 or 6 to high-flying stocks selling at PEs of 50 or 60.

Besides a company's ability to make profits and produce good earnings for its stockholders, the other major consideration in determining its real value has to do with its assets.

The best way to think of *book value* is this: How much money would stockholders get (per share) if a company were to sell all its assets, pay all its debts, and close down its business. If our previously described company has total assets (plant, equipment, inventory, real estate, etc.) valued at $300 million and debts totaling $200 million, then its total net value is $100 million. Dividing this by its 5 million shares of stock, we get a book value of $20 per share. If a share is selling for $18, then the stock of this company is currently selling at a price slightly below its intrinsic value. The relationship between a stock's price and its book value is a widely used measurement of desirability. In 1982 there were many stocks selling well below book value, although the average NYSE company was trading at about book value. The 1983 investor found it much more difficult to discover stocks well below book value.

Return on equity is a term used to express the relationship between a company's earnings and its book value. Our company has earnings of $10 million ($2 per share) and a book value of $100 million ($20 per share), so its return on equity is 10 percent. Look for low PEs and lower-than-book-value prices, but look for a high return on equity. The average NYSE stock earned about 18 percent return on equity in 1982 and 10 percent in 1983.

Earnings per share, PE ratio, book value, and return on equity are just a few of the more commonly used measurements of a stock's value. You may hear your broker use any of these terms. Other considerations that you might think of when choosing a stock are these: management, growth of the industry, innovation and marketing capabilities, volatility of the stock, and how much dividend it pays.

There are dozens of theories and tips about how to make money in the stock market. Every broker and every money manager has a particular style. Here is some of the common advice given to novices that you might keep in mind for an IRA account:

1. Have a goal and stick with it.
2. Cut your losses early; keep winners longer.
3. Diversify.
4. Be objective. Don't keep a stock just because you know the company or because you inherited it.
5. Keep informed, but don't act on rumors.
6. Put only your risk money in the market.
7. Look for undervalued, low-multiple stocks selling below book value.
8. Invest—don't speculate.

My last word about stocks is really the only advice you'll ever need to be a successful investor. It's the oldest investment adage in the world: *Buy low and sell high.* As obvious as this simple rule may sound, most small investors do just the opposite. As a broker, I see it all the time. After watching the stock averages drop continuously for a long period of time, many investors get discouraged and throw in the towel at the very bottom of the market, saying that stocks just have too much risk. After the market has run back up over a long period of time, I often hear from the same investors again, who want to buy back in because they feel that the market is finally safe again.

Buy on bad news. Go in and buy after everyone else has given up and wants to get out at any price. Then *sell on good news.* Sell when everything looks great and everyone is coming back into the market again. The charts show certain patterns that seem to repeat

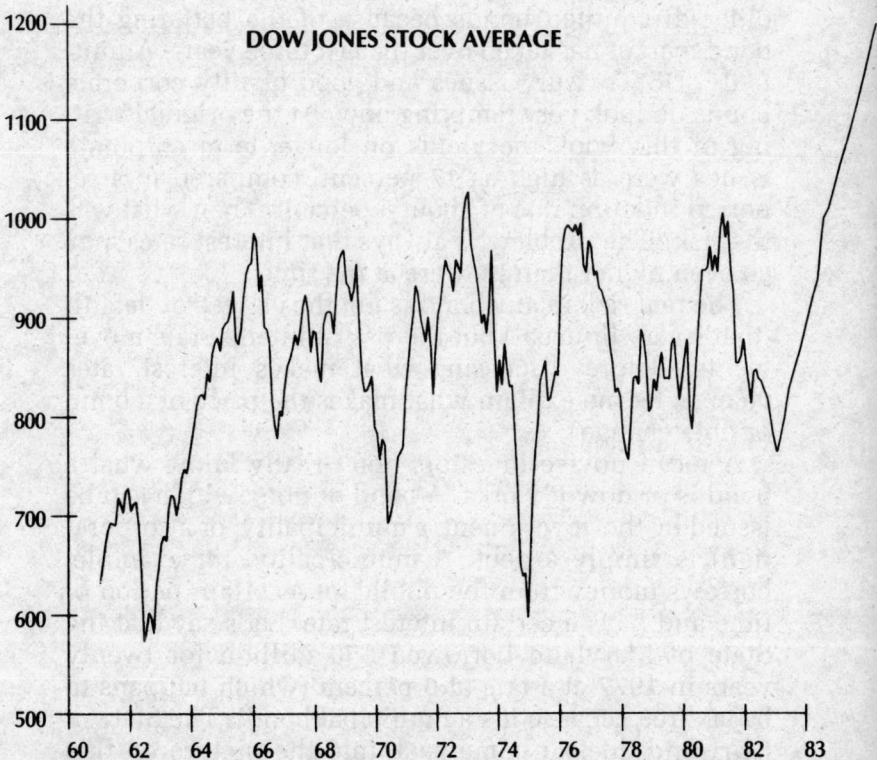

DOW JONES STOCK AVERAGE

themselves. Look at the buying and selling opportunities in the Dow Jones Average over the past twenty years. The greatest buying opportunity was obviously in 1974, when almost everyone was totally pessimistic and finally gave up. Hundreds of stocks doubled and tripled in value in 1975.

BONDS FOR IRAs

Should you buy bonds in your self-directed IRA account? Many investment advisers feel that early 1982 (the first days of the new IRAs) was the best opportunity we have ever had to lock into bonds of any type, because the yields were the highest in history. Also, the reasoning goes, there are still tremendous values in older discounted bonds because of the battering the bond market has taken over the last three years. Admittedly, US Treasury issues and good quality corporate bonds do look very tempting now. At the original writing of this book the yields on longer-term corporate issues were as high as 17 percent, compared to a reported inflation rate of about 8 percent. Then what was the risk? The problem is always that interest rates may go even higher than they are at the time.

The real risk in any bond is not the chance of default (that's very unusual) but the risk of interest-rate movements. Before discussing what makes interest rates change, let me explain what makes the price of a bond or note change.

A lot of novice investors don't really know what a bond is or how it works. A bond or note (which can be issued by the government, a municipality, or a corporation) is simply a debt. A municipality, for example, borrows money from the public for a certain period of time and pays a certain interest rate. Let's say that the State of Maryland borrowed $50 million for twenty years in 1977 at a rate of 6 percent (which happens to be tax free because it's a municipal bond). The State of Maryland doesn't come back into the picture on this particular bond until the maturity date, which is in

1997. Until then the bonds may change hands many times by being bought and sold in the open bond market. The value of this bond at any given time will be determined by what interest rate it's paying (6 percent) compared to what rate other similar bonds (AAA-rated, 20-year municipals in this case) are currently paying. If, for example, Maryland has just issued another bond in 1982, also due to mature in 1997 but paying 12 percent interest, then who wants to buy yours, which you bought five years earlier, which pays only 6 percent interest? Someone will buy it, but not at the same price you originally paid. The value of this bond would be approximately $500 for every $1,000 bond, because that's the price that would make a 6 percent yield equivalent to the going rate of 12 percent.

However, if interest rates start falling over the next few years, the person who bought this year's 12 percent Maryland issue or your discounted 6 percent issue will make a profit. Let's say that two years from now interest rates are back down and Maryland finds itself needing more money again. It issues another bond due in 1997, this time at the going rate of 9 percent. What do you think that 6 percent issue would be worth then? Probably about $750, since that is the price that would give it a yield equivalent to the going rate of 9 percent. The buyer of your discounted 6 percent bond today would then profit some 50 percent in principal (if he buys it from you at $500 and sells it two years from now at $750), in addition to having received tax-free income during those two years.

So the real question with bonds, notes, or any kind of fixed income is which way interest rates are going. If you think rates are going up or if you just don't want to take any risk, then stay very liquid with a daily money market fund. If rates do go up and you are locked into a fixed-rate bond, at best you will be earning less interest than you could be getting, and at worst you could take a big principal loss (as did the first investor in our example) if you had to sell before maturity.

Some people actually think interest rates will never come back down. Their reasoning is that over time, the trend of rates has always been up. Consider the following graph:

LONG-TERM INTEREST RATES
(Yield on 20 years US Government Bonds)

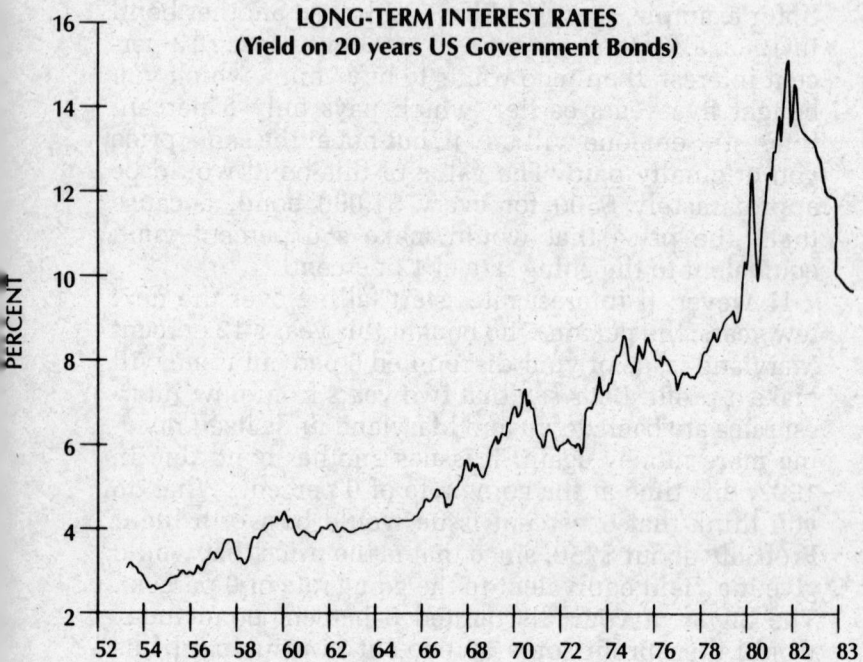

What Makes Interest Rates Change?

If you knew which way interest rates were going to go, you wouldn't be concerned with IRAs, much less a basic guide to the subject. Guessing right on interest rates can be very profitable in almost any of the financial markets.

The fact is that no one knows what interest rates are going to do. There are dozens of theories; but no economist, no banker, and no investment adviser knows for sure which way interest rates will turn next. Ask ten experts and you'll get ten different answers with ten different good reasons.

But there are theories. Since the whole issue of investing for income with bonds centers around what interest rates are going to do, it's important to know about some of the things that are considered to affect the movement of rates. Why, for example, did interest rates stay very high in 1981 and 1982 while the inflation rate came down well below its previous highs?

The investment community says that the cause of high interest rates is the huge federal deficit, citing the enormous borrowing that the government must do to finance this debt, which drives up the demand for money.

Another group says that the deficit has no effect on interest rates. They say that the money supply cannot be controlled and that the only way to control interest rates is to go back on the gold standard. This "supply side" theory says that the interest-rate problem really represents a lack of faith in our currency, which would be corrected by backing that currency with gold.

While "Keynesian theorists" (adherents of John Maynard Keynes's economic theories) focus on the deficit, the "monetarists" say that it is not the deficit itself but the way the deficit is financed (or monetized) that affects both inflation and interest rates. Much has been written about the Federal Reserve's "tight monetary policy." This year the Fed is willing to let interests rates stay high in order to combat inflation.

There are plenty of other interest-rate theories and solutions. But if you are a bond investor, only one thing is important: A buyer of any kind of bond (particularly in an IRA plan) must believe that interest rates will finally come back down and remain at reasonable levels.

MONEY MARKET FUNDS FOR IRAs

The money market funds are the most universally popular investment that the brokerage industry has ever offered. In fact, *Business Week* has said that money market funds "may be the single most important development ever to come along in the financial markets." With soaring interest rates in the late 1970s and early 1980s, the small investor finally found a safe and inexpensive way to participate while maintaining complete liquidity.

Much to the outrage of the tightly regulated banking and thrift industries, some $230 billion was held in more than 180 money market funds by late 1982. The graph that follows shows the skyrocketing popularity of these funds.

Growth of Money Market Funds
1977–1982 Yearends

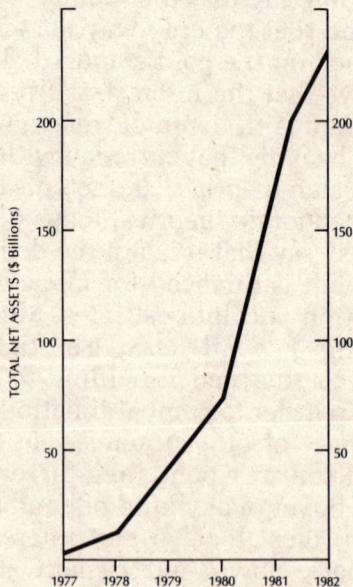

Money market funds are actually a special type of mutual fund that invests only in very short-term (30- to 50-day maturities) money market instruments, such as Treasury bills, bank CDs, and commercial paper (short-term loans to corporations). Investors buy in and sell out of the fund at $1 per share and pay no transaction fee. The interest is figued daily, based on how much the fund is able to earn on its investments. The almost two hundred funds now available are offered by mutual fund companies, insurance companies, brokerage firms, and independent money market fund companies.

Even though the investor is not charged a commission for going in and out of a money market fund, these funds are highly profitable for the companies that sponsor them. As with all mutual funds, the sponsor company takes a small percentage of the income generated by the fund in return for managing the portfolio. Even though the management fee may be only ¼ to ⅜ of 1 percent, the immense size of these portfolios is what makes them so profitable. Consider this: a $10 billion fund (not an unusual size) that charges just ¼ of 1 percent (not an unusual fee) makes $25 million a year in management fees on that one fund alone. (The same company probably sponsors several other mutual funds, too.) The investor never even sees the fee. Instead of getting the 15¼ percent yield that a portfolio might actually produce, for example, the investor would simply get 15 percent while the sponsor keeps the other ¼ percent. Not surprisingly, the number of companies in the money market fund business has soared in recent years. In 1974 there were just fifteen sponsors, and today there are almost two hundred.

The brokerage money market funds are a big advantage to the self-directed IRA investor. They are a place to keep money when it is not invested in other securities. When you sell a stock, for example, and don't want to reinvest immediately, your broker can put your proceeds in a daily money market fund until you do reinvest. If you want to buy bonds but don't think rates have reached their peak yet, you can stay liquid in the money market fund until you want to lock in a bond rate.

I would not recommend using a self-directed plan solely for the purpose of investing in a broker's money market fund, however. If you don't think you'll be investing in other securities, you can avoid the self-directed fees by using a mutual fund or independent money-market fund for your IRA. These custodians charge only a few dollars a year for IRA fees, compared to as much as eighty dollars for the self-directed plans.

OTHER SELF-DIRECTED IRA INVESTMENTS

Your broker may recommend other IRA-appropriate investments for your self-directed plan. Without going into a lot of detail on each one, here is a brief description of some of the more popular IRA investments this year:

1. The zero coupon bond is a recent investment creation that is being touted by the brokerage industry this year for IRA accounts. Instead of paying a fixed interest rate (coupon) like most bonds, these instruments are issued at a discounted price and mature at par value ($1,000); in the meantime, they pay no interest. The advantage of the zero coupon is that you don't have to deal with small interest payments twice a year and that your money continues to grow at the constant rate that you began with (a benefit only if interest rates decline).

If you are considering zero coupon bonds, be sure you compare their true yield-to-maturity with other coupon-paying bonds. Hearing that you can triple your money in twelve years with almost no risk sounds good. But ask what that comes down to in actual yield per year. If it's only 10 percent, for example, and you can get that same yield in a twelve-year Treasury bond, then the zero coupon is no big advantage.

2. Unit trusts are pools of like securities grouped together and sold in units (usually for $1,000 each). Started by the brokers in the mid-seventies, they were originally made up of either municipal or corporate bonds. Since then they have added preferred stock trusts, utility stock trusts, short-term bond trusts, CD trusts, Ginnie Mae trusts, and now even zero coupon bond trusts.

Unlike mutual funds, the unit trust does not alter its portfolio by buying and selling securities. The portfolio is fixed, but the units may be bought and sold by the investors. While these investment trusts do offer the investor some diversification, the cost for this neat packaging is a higher than usual fee.

3. Real estate partnerships are now available for your IRA plan and are appropriate for those who believe in long-term inflation. Ordinarily it wouldn't make sense to buy real estate for an account that is already tax sheltered, but some brokers are now offering partnerships that are designed specifically for retirement accounts. They buy properties for cash (rather than using mortgages), which reduces risk, increases income, and eliminates some of the unneeded tax benefits.

However attractive real estate may have been in the 1970s, investors should be aware that the economic climate of the 1980s is very different. The reason for the soaring real estate prices of the seventies was a combination of high inflation (rising replacement costs) and low interests rates (easy financing). At this writing we have the opposite in both inflation and interest rates, and real estate investments are considered much riskier in general.

Other real estate partnerships for IRA accounts use their funds for financing other people's properties rather than buying their own. By lending their money for completed commercial buildings, the investors get a predictable yield as well as a percentage of the property appreciation and rent increases over the years.

4. Treasury notes and bank CDs can be bought in your

self-directed IRA. Brokers shop for CD rates offered by the major banks and buy them for their clients' accounts with a variety of maturity dates and little or no fee. Treasury bills, notes, and bonds may also be bought for any maturity date with almost no fee for any amount.

5. Annuities and mutual funds that are sponsored by a brokerage firm may be recommended to you for your self-directed plan. Be sure to look at these investments objectively, comparing them to other annuities and funds that are offered by insurance companies and mutual fund groups (see the next two chapters). Keep in mind that if you buy either of these products within a self-directed plan, you will pay two separate fees: one for the investment and one for the plan itself. If the insurance company or mutual fund company acts as the custodian for the IRA plan, however, you will incur just a single fee.

But performance is the most important criterion for any investment. Ask your broker what you get with the proposed annuity or how the proposed mutual fund has performed over the past five or ten years.

Self-Directed IRAs
Comparison of Brokerage Firm Plans

BROKERAGE HOUSE	INITIAL	MINIMUM ANNUAL	COMMISSIONS*
Dean Witter	$20	$20	$54.15
Bache	$25	$50	$53.00
Shearson	None	$50	$53.50
E. F. Hutton	None	$25	$55.00
Kidder Peabody	$25	$25	$54.81
Legg Mason	$25	$25	$52.17
Paine Webber	$25	$25	$53.50
Alex Brown	$25	$35	$49.46

*What it costs to buy or sell 100 shares @ $20/shr.

Investments to Avoid

There are three categories of investments that should be avoided in your self-directed IRA account: Those that are not allowed, those that are not logical, and those that are too risky.

Commodity futures of any type are not allowed in an IRA account. They're considered too risky. The IRS also disallowed, last year, the use of collectibles for IRA accounts. Collectibles include things like metals, art, stamps, and other nonsecurity investments. The reason for this disallowance, as mentioned earlier, is that many people were using IRA money to decorate their homes under the old IRA rules.

It would be foolish to use investments that are normally bought for their tax advantages in an IRA account. It would not be logical, for example, to buy the Maryland municipal bond, cited earlier, in your self-directed IRA account. Municipal bond yields are lower than other bond yields because the interest is tax free on municipals. Since you don't pay current taxes on any IRA investment anyway, you should simply look for the best return you can get regardless of the normal tax treatment.

ACT AS OWN TRUSTEE	HAVE IN-HOUSE MONEY MARKET FUND
yes	yes
no	yes
yes	yes
no	yes
no	yes
no	yes
no	no
no	yes

Tax shelters, such as oil- and gas-drilling programs, which give you deductions against your own earned income to compensate for their high risk, would make even less sense than municipal bonds for IRAs. Since you can't deduct the same amount of money twice, using your already deducted IRA contributions for a high-risk, illiquid venture while forgoing its normal tax benefit is clearly not prudent investing. The same would be true for any other tax-advantaged investment.

Finally, always keep risk in mind. Remember that an IRA is a retirement account and is not meant for speculation. Some investments, such as buying options, are allowed for IRAs but not recommended.

The Case for Equities

John M. Templeton gave a speech in New York on January 27, 1982, to a group of financial writers in which he predicted that the Dow Jones Average will go to 3,000 sometime within the next seven years. Such a prediction would normally not get that much attention, except for the fact that it was John Templeton who said it. Widely respected as one of Wall Street's best money managers of all time, Mr. Templeton's Growth Fund and World Fund have both demonstrated enormous growth over the years (see the performance tables of mutual funds in the next chapter).

I asked Mr. Templeton for permission to reprint this now famous speech because I think he presents a good argument for the whole strategy of investing in equities for long-term growth at this time. He makes some very clear and convincing arguments about how underpriced most stocks were at the time. Given the market's spectacular rise since the time of this speech, few doubts of his ability can remain.

1. Let's start out with the fact that the price/earnings ratios of American stocks are now unusually low. Depending on which analyst you are reading, you will come out with a price/earnings ratio of about seven, in relation to today's market prices and the estimates of earnings for 1982. Those of you who are historians of American stock markets will know that throughout the last ninety years, the average price has been fourteen times earnings. Average obviously means that fifty percent of the time in the last ninety years, price/ earnings ratios were higher than fourteen. Probably someday we will get back to the average. It would seem quite likely that at some time you'll be able to say again that stock prices are fourteen times earnings. That's the first point.

  2. **The second point is what will happen to earnings?** Now earnings are dependent on sales volume, and sales volume is dependent partly on inflation. I believe that inflation is going to continue. There's no nation in the world that doesn't have inflation. I don't believe that in my lifetime or the lifetime of any of you, you will ever see a year of deflation. By deflation, I mean a decline in the cost of living. I don't think there will be a year when you will be able to say that your money will buy more than what it bought a year earlier. My best estimates are that over the next ten years we may be fortunate enough to have a year in which we have only 3% inflation. On the other hand, there will be times when we have 20% inflation in the United States, averaging out to about 9%. Now that is provided we don't have a catastrophe. If we have a catastrophe such as a war or electing a socialist, or other such catastrophes, we'll have more inflation. Also, 90% of the nations in the world will have more inflation than the United States. If you say we're going to average 9% inflation that's the same as saying that the sales volume of corporations will double in eight years, even if they don't produce any more goods. Nine percent a year for eight years compounded doubles the sales volume. Now, obviously, during that period corporations will produce more goods. So let's say that the sales volume of American corporations will double in seven years. I think I'm being conservative in that; I would say in all probability, it will be less than seven years.

  Now if the sales volume doubles and the profit margin stays the same, then the profits double. So if you're looking seven years ahead and the profits have doubled and the price/earnings ratio is normal again then you'll have share prices four times as high as they are now. A doubling in earnings and a doubling in the price/ earnings ratio. And, as you all know, four times today's price would be well above 3,000 on the Dow Jones Industrial Average. We do not know whether prices will be higher or lower in 1982; but chances do appear better than even that some day within the next seven years, the the Dow Jones Industrial Average may rise above 3,000.

3. The third point is that the possibility of reaching 3,000 on the Dow is confirmed when you look at what has happened in other nations. Already price/earnings ratios in Singapore are approximately 20 times earnings. In Japan about 23 times earnings. Most nations of the world have price/earnings ratios higher now than the United States although I do believe that the problems of the United States are smaller than those of many other nations.

Now there are many articles written by wise economists who will tell you that price/earnings ratios cannot be high as long as interest rates are high and no doubt that is an influence. When you're able to buy tax-free bonds now to yield 14% and when inflation last year was 9% then you have a genuine, real yield on those tax-free bonds of 5%. So that represents a competition with share prices and it does cause lower share prices than might be otherwise.

But the point is that if you make your investment studies worldwide, you would find that high interest rates—high returns on bonds—do not prevent high price/earnings ratios. There are examples at present and numerous examples in history where high yields on bonds occurred at the same time as high price/earnings ratios and for many different reasons. The biggest reason is fear. When investors are frightened that they are going to lose the purchasing power of their money, they will buy assets such as real estate and common stocks at high prices, because they are just afraid to buy bonds or mortgages or anything fixed in terms of the currency. Examples can be found in Europe, South America, or Asia where high interest rates occurred at the same time as high price/earnings ratios.

My point is that we may continue to have high interest rates but this may not prevent us from also returning at some time to average price/earnings ratios of 14 times.

4. My next point concerns how high United States share prices are in relation to book value. Up until three years ago, there had been only three times in the history of the Dow Jones Industrial Average when prices were below book value; and all three of those times proved to be very short and wonderful times to load up on common stocks. Of course, one of those was in the great depression in 1932. Another was at the time when it looked as if the United States might lose the war in 1942, and another was in 1948. All of those proved to be excellent buying opportunities for American common stocks. Now share prices again are well below book values. We don't know the exact book values at the moment for the year just ended, but they are in the neighborhood of a thousand, on the thirty stocks that make up the Dow Jones Average, as compared with stock market values 16% lower than that. So we are 16% below book values and by historical performance, that is a favorable time to buy.

5. Next, let me comment on replacement book value—something that I recommend all of you study. It's amazing that so little attention has been given to replacement book value. Because of inflation, it costs more to build a corporation than shows on the corporation balance sheet and, at present, that figure is something like 70% more. So approximately 70% above stated book value is the replacement value which, at present, would be about 1,700 on the Dow Jones Average. So the Dow Jones Average is selling for less than half of the replacement value. The striking thing that I've seen very rarely mentioned is that on the worst day of the greatest depression in history, in June 1932—when the Dow Jones Average had declined from 360 in 1929 down to only 42 on the worst day—on that day it was still not as cheap in relation to replacement book value as it is right now today.

6. Now another reason why I think share prices are likely to be much higher is that never have we seen so many acquisitions. The people who are buying a corporation have appraised its value and they feel they're getting a bargain when they buy that corporation. The prices they pay in these acquisitions and takeovers are often surprisingly high. You yourselves have seen many takeovers at 50%, even 100%, above the price at which that stock was selling on the exchange. That's an indication to me that share prices are obviously cheap at present.

7. [The] next point is that never in history have we seen so many corporations buying in their own shares. This also is an indication that the shares are selling at low prices. When the directors meet, they have a choice between using their cash to build another factory or to buy in their own shares. But when their shares are selling at a half or less of the replacement cost, obviously, they are wiser to buy in their own shares. This is a further indication that share prices are extraordinarily low. Five or ten years from now, we may all look back at these days as the good old bargain days when we should have loaded up on common stocks.

8. Another indication of the potential in share prices is found by looking back at American share price history. In 1966 the Dow Jones Industrial Average reached 996. It's now roughly 840. So prices of the 30 stocks in the index are lower than they were sixteen years ago. This is an unusual situation and it has not happened in many other nations. Share prices in Canada are double what they were at that time. Share prices in England, which has had much worse problems than the United States, are three times as high as they were then. Share prices in Japan are five times as high as they were then. But in the United States, this share price index is lower than it was sixteen years ago.

Sixteen years ago, we had just gone through the longest, greatest bull market in the history of the Dow Jones Index. From 1949 to 1966 share prices had gone up five times where they had been—that was a high point. So after having gone up to five times where they were, it's not too surprising that in the next sixteen years they went nowhere. But if we have another repetition of that bull market then it's conceivable in the next sixteen years that share prices could again go up to five times what they were. I don't consider that unreasonably optimistic because in those days, you didn't have much inflation; whereas now and in the future, we're going to have more inflation. So it's more likely in the next sixteen years than it was in those sixteen years that ended in 1966.

9. Now lastly, let us turn to an entirely different subject to illustrate where share prices may go. All I've said so far is in terms of history and values, but the more important side is who is going to do the buying? Where's the cash? Share prices can remain low for a long, long time if nobody wants to buy. But when you look around today, more cash is available to buy common stocks than ever before.

One source of cash is pension funds. Thirty years ago there was very little money in pensions funds; now between six hundred billion and seven hundred billion dollars is held in pension funds. Those of you who are in the pension fund business have read predictions that within fifteen years, the private pension funds in the United States will be three trillion dollars. The private plus the public pension funds, a few experts have said, will be as high as five trillion dollars. But let's take the lower figure, to be conservative, of three trillion dollars and ask how much of that will go into common stocks. Throughout the history of pension funds, common stocks have averaged 55%. There have been occasional years when more than 100% of the new contributions went into common stocks. The tendency is for pension funds to put more in common stocks, not less. For example, General Motors Corporation announced publicly that their pension funds will move from 50% normally in stocks to 70%.

So the trend is toward more stocks but, again, to be conservative, let's say that fifteen years from now the pension funds have only 50% in common stocks. Fifty percent of three trillion is one and a half trillion dollars. But how many common stocks are there? In the United States, at this moment, there are only one and a quarter trillion dollars worth of common stocks. So, theoretically, the pension funds alone might buy up more than 100% of all the outstanding stocks. Now, obviously, that isn't going to happen; it's impossible. But this does illustrate my point that we may be surprised in the next six, seven or eight years to see how high share prices rise. There can develop a shortage of shares.

As to another source of cash, last July the government changed the tax laws so that now every person who has earned income can set up for himself his own pension fund called an "Individual Retirement Account." Those of you who are in the financial business know that is an enormous opportunity. The mutual fund salesmen, the savings banks, and many others are pointing out to the people that all they have to do is to set up their own IRA, put two thousand dollars in it; they can subtract that two thousand dollars from their top tax bracket and invest it so that all earnings and gains are tax-free until they retire. That's such an enormous advantage; it's hard for me to imagine any American that won't do that. It would take a man that didn't know what he was doing to refuse an offer like that.

There are a hundred million people who are eligible for IRA. Suppose that only one-quarter of them put their money into these IRA's. That's twenty-five million people; and two thousand dollars times twenty-five million is fifty billion dollars per year. Let's suppose only half of that goes into common stocks. That's twenty-five billion dollars of new money each year going into common stocks. But, that's much more than the new supply of common stocks coming into the market each year. So the Individual Retirement Accounts can have a very large effect in pushing share prices up.

This is one of the great things—this may go down in economic history as one of the great changes in America—the beginning of people's capitalism. Instead of having only thirty-three million people in the country who own shares, we may soon find sixty million people who own shares. As we're told, "Where your treasure is, there will your heart be also." When you have your money in common stocks, you gradually educate yourself on the meaning of private enterprise and on the problems of business. You're likely to be more intelligent when you go to the voting booth. So this change in the tax policy last July is going to have a permanent, long-range effect on the economy of the United States; and I believe it will be a change all for the good. Instead of hating your boss, how can you hate the boss when you own the company yourself. So I believe we are coming into a period of harmony and a period of prosperity—a period that we'll look back on as a great turning point in the prosperity of the nation.

10

Mutual Fund Plans

The mutual fund industry expects to increase its stake in IRA business from 3 percent of total pre-1982 IRA assets to over 30 percent. Like the brokerage and insurance companies, mutual fund companies never went after IRA accounts aggressively until last year.

The funds to have a convincing argument for IRA investors. They seem to have everything you would want in a small investment account: diversification and flexibility, relative safety, professional management, liquidity, low fees, automatic reinvestment of income and gains, and good potential for growth. It's easy to find out which funds have performed well and which ones haven't by referring to any of the numerous services that track the funds. Most funds do offer IRA accounts and can be purchased in very small increments.

While the depository plans may be the best place for most first-time investors to put their IRA money, the mutual funds may be the most suitable place for the slightly more aggressive or experienced investor particularly in the first few years of contributions. Today more than 20 million investors own shares of mutual funds.

How Does a Mutual Fund Work?

A mutual fund is simply an investment management company through which an individual can purchase a well-diversified portfolio of securities. The small investor pools money with thousands of other people in order to get this diversity and professional supervision.

Your shares of the fund represent a cross section of the fund's entire portfolio: perhaps a hundred different stocks or bonds. The value of your fund shares is determined not by demand for the fund itself but rather by the value of the securities in the fund. In other words, it's possible that a fund could shrink in size (due to the redemption of shares) yet increase in price per share (due to good portfolio performance) at the same time. The price of a mutual fund share is called its *net asset value* and is determined simply by dividing the total portfolio value by the current number of shares that make up the fund. If the actual value of a fund's portfolio on a given day were exactly $100 million, for example, and the number of shares outstanding happened to be exactly 4 million (what a coincidence), then the price of that fund would be $25 per share that day. Most funds are priced at the end of each day and are listed in the next day's newspapers under a special section on mutual funds.

Every mutual fund has a manager (either an individual or a team) who is solely responsible for its performance. The fund manager continually watches the portfolio and makes changes as he or she sees fit; the manager has total discretion to buy and sell securities for the fund.

There are over seven hundred mutual funds today.

They can be categorized by their investment objectives: growth funds, income funds, balanced funds, and money market funds.

Growth funds buy common stocks for capital appreciation. Each fund has a slightly different approach to reaching its goals in this highly competitive and highly visible industry. Some funds are very aggressive and buy shares of younger, emerging companies, while other funds stay with only blue-chip stocks. Some portfolio managers search international markets, while others specialize in particular industries. But their common objective is to beat the averages: the inflation rate, the stock indexes, the money market rates, and, most important, the other funds.

Income funds buy notes, bonds, and preferred stocks as well as shorter-term instruments. Achieving high income without losing principal has been no easy task in recent years as interest rates have soared. These fixed-income managers are continuously trying to juggle portfolio mix and maturity dates to protect that principal, since their performance is also measured by total investment value from year to year. Income funds are bought mainly by people who need to use the income (many are retirees), although dividends and interest can be plowed back into the fund in reinvested shares.

Balanced funds are portfolios made up of a combination of growth and income securities. Their objective is to provide enough income for people who depend on it but also to achieve portfolio growth through their common-stock investments.

By far the largest influx of mutual fund money has been in the area of *money market funds*. Over $100 billion of new money was deposited into the funds in 1981 alone. With interest rates as high as 20 percent, combined with liquidity and safety, it's no mystery why these funds became so universally popular.

A *family of funds* is a mutual fund company (group)

that offers at least one growth fund, one income fund, and a money market fund. The investor can easily and inexpensively switch from one fund to another just by making a phone call. This flexibility is particularly handy for IRA accounts and will be discussed in more detail later (see page 144).

The mutual fund company makes its profits by charging a small management fee based on a percentage of the assets it manages. One half of one percent is a typical charge made by the larger funds. It is simply deducted from the income generated in the portfolio.

Mutual funds are as liquid as individual stocks and bonds, although the normal procedure for redemption is to submit your request in writing rather than doing it by phone. If you want to get your money out of a fund, whether it is in an IRA plan or just in your own name, write to the address of the place that sends you your quarterly statements and include (1) your certificate (if it was ever sent to you); (2) a "stock power" form with your signature guaranteed (form and guarantee can be gotten from your banker or broker); and (3) a note saying the following: "Dear Sirs: Please redeem all full and partial shares of my [name of fund] in account number [your number] and send the proceeds directly to me at [address]" I mention this simple procedure because there is so much confusion about mutual fund liquidations. As you might expect, the funds make it a lot easier to get in than to get out.

Load vs. No-Load Funds

Of the approximately seven hundred mutual funds available today, about half charge a commission to buy them and about half don't.

No-load funds charge no commissions to purchase them, although a few charge a slightly higher annual management fee and some have a redemption charge of up to 2 percent. Since these funds have no marketing organization, you must contact the company directly for information about what they are offering.

Load funds are sold through agents and stockbrokers and do charge a commission for purchase, which normally ranges for 1 percent to 8½ percent depending on the type of fund and the amount purchased. There is no charge to sell a load fund. Shares of these funds are quoted for both buy and sell prices, much like the bid-and-offer prices of an individual stock or bond.

The costs involved in any mutual fund, load or no-load, are actually very low for what you get. Let's compare them to what it costs to buy or sell an individual stock. If you are considering the purchase of a $20 stock, for example, you may find that it is currently bidding 19½ (the most anyone is willing to pay for it at the time) and asking 20 (the least anyone is willing to sell if for). When you buy the stock, you will be charged a commission of approximately 2½ percent (for a small purchase), making your total cost about $20.50 for each share. If you were to sell this stock at the same price, you would probably only get 19½, minus a commission, leaving you with only about $19.00. The total cost of going in and out of this one stock, figuring in the bid-and-offer "spread" as well as the two commissions, could be 7 or 8 percent. You'd better hope that the stock goes up in price.

With a mutual fund, however, your costs over a period of time can be much lower than buying and selling individual stocks. The buy and sell prices of a load fund might also be 7 or 8 percent ($19 to sell and $20.50 to buy), but that's your total cost as long as you are in the fund. Transactions made within the fund by the portfolio manager are absorbed by the fund itself at a fraction of normal commissions per share because of the size of the transactions being made. If you hold your fund for a few years or more, which is what most people do, your portfolio may be turned over several times. Your eventual savings are particularly signifi-

cant in an IRA account because these small transactions that you would make on your own for individual securities are the costliest.

The most important thing in choosing a mutual fund
is to get a fund that has had a good long-term performance record. Over time, fees don't make a bit of difference if the fund continues to perform well. The 7 percent initial fee that Templeton Growth Fund charged a
$10,000 investor ten years ago looks minuscule now,
after an 850 percent increase in value has turned that
investment into $85,000.

How to Pick a Mutual Fund for Your IRA

Fortunately there are many accessible and objective
sources of information on mutual fund performance.

The reports tell us that of the $250 billion now in-
vested in mutual funds, the vast majority of it is doing a
lot better than if it were being managed by the individuals who put it into the funds. Over the past twenty
years the average balanced fund (combination growth
and income) has gone up in value some 450 percent,
compared to a total increase of 189 percent in the Consumer Price Index over the same period. The top
twelve funds averaged a 37 percent annual return for
the 1970s, which included some very difficult years in
the stock market.

But how do you find which specific funds have been
the leaders? Among the most widely followed mutual
fund reporting services are: Lipper Analytical Services,
Wiesenberger Investment Companies Services, Johnson's Investment Company Charts, and United Business Services. *Forbes* magazine also conducts an extensive annual survey that is published in its August
issue.

Each year some specialized group of funds will turn
in a great performance, while the leading group from
the year before may alredy be in a downswing. The

gold funds had their heyday a few years ago but then fizzled out as the price of gold plummeted. Funds that specialized in energy and technology stocks had similar (but not as dramatic) cycles in recent years. Many funds look good from time to time or under certain market conditions. But consistency over a long period of time, through adverse market conditions as well as favorable ones, is what the investor must find for IRA funds.

According to *Money* magazine, the following were the top ten funds for total return over the past year:

Mutual Funds
One Year Performance

Fund (load, if any)	Type	% GAIN THROUGH APRIL 1983			
		ONE YEAR	RANK	FIVE YEARS	RANK
United Services Gold Shares	Gold	142.0	1	671.6	1
Fidelity Select—Precious Metals	Gold	122.6	2	—	—
Fidelity Select—Technology	Growth	119.9	3	—	—
Strategic Investments (8½%)	Gold	117.8	4	620.7	2
Oppenheimer Target (6%)	Max. Cap. Gain	102.5	5	—	—
Twentieth Century Ultra (1%)	Max. Cap. Gain	93.9	6	—	—
Hartwell Leverage	Max. Cap. Gain	91.0	7	350.4	8
Franklin Research Capital (7¼%)	Gold	90.8	8	508.0	5
First Investors Discovery (8½%)	Max. Cap. Gain	88.0	9	198.3	58
Fidelity Magellan (3%)	Max. Cap. Gain	87.8	10	550.8	3

Since IRA investors are concerned with even longer-term performance, here are the Johnson Charts results for 10, 15, 20, and 25 years (based on the 1982 report):

10 Year Performances

1. Twentieth Century Growth Investors
2. Templeton Growth Fund
3. Evergreen Fund
4. Mutual Shares Corp
5. Pioneer II Fund

15 Year Performances

1. Fidelity Magellan Fund
2. Templeton Growth Fund
3. Mutual Shares Corp.
4. Twentieth Century Growth Investors
5. Mathers Fund, Inc.

20 Year Performances

1. Templeton Growth
2. Mutual Shares
3. Twentieth Century Growth Investors
4. Over the Counter Security Inc.
5. American General Enterprise

25 Year Performances

1. Over the Counter Security
2. Templeton Growth
3. Mutual Shares
4. Scudder Special Fund, Inc.
5. American General Enterprise

How a fund performs in bad markets is extremely important to investors concerned with safety of principal. *Forbes* uses its own rating system for measuring both good-market and bad-market performances. Their system is now widely referred to as a measurement of safety.

The magazine's latest "honor roll," which covers three bull markets and three bear markets over a twelve-year period, is as follows:

FUND	TYPE	MARKET RATINGS	
		BULL	BEAR
AMCAP	Load	A	B
American General Comstock	Load	B	A
American General Pace	Load	A+	A
Charter	Load	A+	B
Fidelity Magellan	Load	A+	B
International Investors	Load	A	A
Janus	No-load	A	A
Mutual Shares	No-load	B	B
Nicholas	No-load	A	B
Pioneer II	Load	B	A
Putnam-Voyager	Load	A	C
St. Paul Growth	Load	A	B
Sigma Venture Shares	Load	A+	C
Templeton Growth	Load	B	B
Twentieth Century Growth	No-load	A+	C
Twentieth Century Select	No-load	A+	B
Vance, Sanders Special	Load	A	C

Keep your eye on your money market yield. Most people failed to respond to the big interest rate drop of 1982–1983, leaving most of their money in cash rather than taking advantage of the soaring stock and bond markets. The following list from *Money* magazine compares money market yields at the time of the original writing of this book to those in April 1983, when the book was revised.

Money Market Funds

	% YIELD	
	APRIL 1983	APRIL 1982
Kemper Money Market	8.4	14.4
Cash Reserve Management	8.3	14.2
MoneyMart Assets	8.3	14.2
Paine Webber Cashfund	8.2	14.0
Shearson Daily Dividend	8.2	14.1
Fidelity Cash Reserves	8.2	14.0
Dreyfus Liquid Assets	8.1	13.9
Dean Witter-Sears L. A.	8.0	13.9
Daily Cash Accumulation	8.0	14.0

Mutual Fund IRAs
Characteristics of 10 of the Best Performing Funds*

MUTUAL FUND	IRA MINIMUMS		IRA FEES		PHONE # TO GET MORE INFORMATION AND AN APPLICATION
	INITIAL	INCRE-MENTS	ANNUAL	TO SWITCH TO ANOTHER FUND IN THE SAME GROUP	
1. Templeton Growth Fund	$500.00	$25.00	$10.00	None	800/237-0738
2. Mutual Shares	$500.00	None	$ 5.00 plus $ 5.00 initial	None	800/221-7864
3. Twentieth Century Growth	$ 25.00	None	$10.00	None	816/531-5575
4. OTC Securities	$ 25.00	$25.00	$ 2.50 plus $ 5.00 initial	None	215/887-3011
5. American General Enterprise	$ 50.00	$50.00	$ 7.50	$5.00	713/526-8561
6. Plitrend Fund	None	None	$ 5.00	$5.00	215/629-9800
7. Financial Industrial Income	None	None	$ 5.00 initial only	None	303/779-1233
8. Value Line Fund, Inc.	$250.00	$25.00	$ 6.00 plus $ 5.25 initial	None	212/687-3965
9. Pioneer Fund, Inc.	$250.00	$25.00	$ 6.00	$5.00	617/742-7825
10. Price (Rowe) New Horizons Fund	$500.00	$50.00	$ 3.00	None	301/547-2136

*According to Johnson's Charts' 20-year list for 1982.

Large Money Market Funds That Offer IRA Plans

		MINIMUM INVESTMENT:		PREDOMINANT SECURITIES IN PORTFOLIO	OTHER INVESTMENT CHOICES:		APPROXIMATE ASSETS, 1982 (BILLIONS)
		INITIALLY	THEREAFTER		GROWTH FUND	BOND OR INCOME FUND	
Alliance Capital Reserves 140 Broadway New York, N.Y. 10005	212-902-4126 800-221-5672	None	None	Commercial paper Bank CDs	✓	No-load funds	1.5
Capital Preservation Fund 755 Page Mill Rd. Palo Alto, Calif. 94304	800-472-3389	None	None	Government			1.9
Current Interest 333 Clay St., Suite 4300 Houston, Texas 77002	800-392-7802 800-231-4645	None	None	Commercial paper	✓	Load funds	1.5
Daily Cash Accumulation P.O. Box 300 Denver, Colo. 80201	303-770-2345 800-525-9310	$250	25	Commercial paper			5.4
Delaware Cash Reserves 10 Penn Center Plaza Philadelphia, Pa. 19103	800-462-1597 800-523-1640	$50	25	Commercial paper Eurodollar CDs	✓	✓ Load funds	2.2
Dreyfus Liquid Assets 600 Madison Ave. New York, N.Y. 10022	212-223-0303 800-223-0982	$750	None	Bank CDs	✓	✓ No-load funds	10.0
Fidelity Cash Reserves 82 Devonshire St. Boston, Mass. 02109	800-392-6097 800-225-6197	$500	250	Commercial paper	✓	✓ No-load funds	3.9

Fund	Phone	Minimum (initial / subsequent)	Investment	Load	Yield
First Variable Rate Gov't. 1700 Pennsylvania Ave. N.W. Washington, D.C. 20006	301-951-4820 800-368-2748	$1,000 / 250	Government		1.4
Fund for Gov't. Investors 1735 K St. N.W. Washington, D.C. 20006	202-861-1800	$500 / None	Government		1.3
InterCapital Liquid Assets Any office of Dean Witter		$1,000 / 100	Commercial paper	✓ Load funds	9.4
Kemper Money Market 120 S. LaSalle St. Chicago, Ill. 60603	312-781-1121 800-621-1048	$250 / 50	Commercial paper	✓ Load funds	3.5
Moneymart Assets Any office of Bache		None / None	Commercial paper	✓ Load funds	3.9
National Liquid Reserves 1345 Ave. of the Americas New York, N.Y. 10105	212-530-1787 800-221-2990	$1,000 / 1	Commercial paper	✓ Load funds	1.9
Oppenheimer Money Market P.O. Box 300 Denver, Colo. 80201	212-668-5100 800-221-9839	$250 / 25	Commercial paper	✓ Load funds	1.6
Reserve Fund—Primary 810 Seventh Ave. New York, N.Y. 10019	212-977-9880 800-223-5547	$250 / 250	Eurodollar CDs	✓ Load funds	2.9
T. Rowe Price Prime Reserve 100 E. Pratt St. Baltimore, Md. 21202	800-492-1976 800-638-5660	$500 / 50	Commercial paper	✓ No-load funds	3.4

Fund Switching

Some mutual fund companies now have several different funds, each with different investment objectives, available within the same group. These are sometimes called a *family of funds*. An investor can switch from one fund to another just by making a phone call.

The family-of-funds approach seems to be one of the best answers to the great financial dilemma of the year—where to stash your IRA money. While interest rates are on the rise and stocks and bonds are falling, you can keep your money safe and liquid in the group's money market fund. If rates start falling and you want to lock in a diversified portfolio of longer-term corporate or government bonds, you can switch some of your funds into that portfolio. And if you feel that stocks have finally hit their bottom, it may be time to switch some funds into the group's stock portfolio. You might even have a choice of several different stock funds, each with a different approach and objective.

If you define a family of funds as a mutual fund group having at least one stock fund, one income fund, and one money market fund, then an IRA investor has some thirty-six companies to choose from, each with an average of six different funds under its management. One group, Fidelity has twenty-five funds in its group to choose from. Many financial planners feel that the mutual fund groups are a good place for IRA money because of the low cost, flexibility, and liquidity.

Even with a passive vehicle such as a mutual fund, there are still investment decisions to be made by the IRA investor. In the family-of-funds switching approach, for example, you must first choose which group to use, then make decisions from time to time about which specific funds to be in. These decisions should be based on the same criteria that you use in any investment choice: your age, income, other investments, temperament, and overall financial goals. The timing and investment strategy in the funds is the same as you would use in a self-directed account: buy when everyone else has given up and the market (any market) looks the worst, then sell just when everyone else feels that it's finally safe again.

Advantages and Disadvantages of Mutual Funds

Jane Bryant Quinn says (in her popular *Everyone's Money Book* [New York: Delacorte Press, 1978]) that "mutual funds are the very best investment vehicle for the average person." The number of mutual fund investors has soared in recent years, mostly because of the popular money market funds. Between the mid 1970s and 1982, total mutual fund assets grew from $50 billion to over $250 billion. In 1981 alone mutual fund assets grew by 70 percent.

Until recently 90 percent of the industry's funds were invested in common stocks. Investing in a mutual fund was synonymous with buying a diversified portfolio of stocks. The sudden explosion of the money market funds simply illustrates a broader application of the basic mutual fund principles: pooling of money and investors, employment of professional money managers, and instant liquidity of investment.

We have already addressed most of the advantages of using mutual funds for your IRA. Most of the funds do offer IRA plans, and applications for them, incidentally, are usually the shortest and simplest of any of the custodian types. Both the annual IRA fees and the switching fees (if any) are very low for all funds. They seem to fit many people's IRA requirement of small minimum amounts, small incremental contributions, and automatic reinvestment of income and gains. In fact, you can generally arrange to have your bank make a regular payment directly to the fund out of your checking or savings account. The flexibility of investment offered by the fund groups is an added advantage.

The safety of mutual funds depends a lot on the type of fund you choose. Aggressive stock funds are certainly riskier than money market funds, for example.

But as a general investment vehicle, mutual funds are relatively safe. The professional guidance, strict government regulations, and broad diversification within each fund all add up to help reduce the investor's risk.

Professional management is no small advantage to the funds. While some skeptics believe only in the "random walk" (luck) theory of investing, there is little question that over time the highly skilled securities analyst should outperform the amateur. Just look at the longer-term performance records of the best mutual funds. Investment managers responsible for billions of dollars can obviously get more timely information and advice from their own industry than can individual investors handling just their own money.

There is plenty of objective information on all the funds available today to help you decide which one is right for you. It is also easy to follow your investment once you buy a fund, because most major newspapers carry a daily list of mutual fund prices.

The funds, of course, are not for everyone. I suggested in an earlier chapter that the majority of first-time investors should probably use a depository institution for their IRA plans. There they have absolutely no risk and no real investment decisions to make. A mutual fund should not be used by the most conservative investor because there is always some element of risk. The funds are usually best suited for investors who have long-term capital growth or long-term total return as an objective, and who don't want to spend a lot of time on their investments. This would also eliminate the self-directed type of investor. Many people really enjoy handling their own investments directly, making each specific decision on their own. This type of investor would find a mutual fund too passive. Also, some people hedge at paying the commission that the load funds charge, even though many of the load funds have had excellent performance records. All these factors should be weighed before making your decision about where to start your IRA plan.

11

Insurance Company Plans

Insurance Woes

Like the depository institutions, this country's life insurance companies have seen hard times in recent years due to high interest rates. Some companies registered tremendous losses in 1981 and 1982, and many analysts feel that the industry itself must reorganize just to survive in the new era of financial competition. The three main problems that the industry faces in the 1980s seem almost insurmountable:

A. Approximately 65 percent of all the corporate debt (bonds) in the United States is currently owned by insurance companies. As everyone knows by now, long-term bonds were a disastrous investment for many years, until interest rates dropped in 1982. It is estimated that the life insurance industry had lost some 38 percent of its collective investment portfolio going into 1982.

The industry's stock and real estate investments haven't done well either. Institutional investors, including insurance company portfolio managers, have had a dismal record over the years, consistently underperforming the averages. And the insurance companies' traditional real estate role (as lender rather than owner) left them stuck with even more long-term, low-interest-rate loans rather than the phenomenal equity buildup that the owners got during the inflationary 1970s.

The industry's unlucky investing will have a tremendous effect on the American capital structure and financial markets for years to come. The costly lesson that the insurers learned about interest rates has probably already changed the long-term debt structure of the country permanently. No longer are the insurance companies willing to pour huge amounts of money into long-term, fixed-rate bonds; many will now lend only for a few years at a time. And no longer will the insurers make huge fixed-rate loans for commercial real estate projects and remain as passive lenders; today they demand to share in the equity. Even residential mortgages today are made on an adjustable-rate basis. Since insurance companies have always been a major source of mortgage money, their new reluctance only adds to the severe problems in today's housing industry.

B. The life insurance industry has been dealt two other severe blows in recent years, both of which result from enhanced consumer awareness. The first is a major trend by insurance policyholders toward borrowing against their policies. The insurance companies are contractually obligated to lend billions of dollars based on these policies at very low interest rates; and every smart consumer knows that this is a bargain. While the industry must lend out this money at 5 percent, it has to borrow at current rates, which may be two or three times as high.

The other consumer trend that has hurt the industry tremendously in recent years is the preference toward *term* insurance over *whole-life* insurance. Whole-life, which is much more profitable to the companies, is a combination insurance and savings plan. Unfortunately, the savings plan is not a very good deal for the policyholder since the interest rate paid is only about 5–6 percent. Most people today are turning to term insurance. This is a much cheaper means of insuring your life without getting tied into a low-yielding savings plan. The company that you work for may cover you with a term insurance policy, for example.

The competition from the new "financial supermarkets" (see Financial Supermarkets, page 35) for insurance business hasn't helped the traditional insurance companies in recent years either. Many of the newcomers have been much more creative in both products and marketing than the older companies, which are now finding that they must adapt fast just to survive.

Insurance products always seem more complicated than those of the other financial institutions. Perhaps this is because of the language of the insurance industry. I have found that the majority of investors have little knowledge about what insurance companies really do: how they fit into the overall financial system; what products and services they offer; and how they make their money. The industry has somehow managed to keep an aura of mystery surrounding it in an age of consumer curiosity.

One thing you do know about insurance companies by now is that they are in the IRA business. Not surprisingly, insurance companies want your IRA dollars just as badly as all the other custodians do. They are offering a special type of retirement annuity that has investment options similar to the mutual fund plans. It is essential to understand what an annuity is in order to compare the IRA choices offered by the insurance industry.

Annuities

Basically an annuity is a promise by an insurance company to pay you income for as long as you live, in return for a lump sum of money that you invest. The amount that the insurer will pay you each year will depend on both your life expectancy and the amount of money you invest. If you live exactly the number of years the actuarians predict, then your entire deposit, plus interest, will be paid back to you during your lifetime.

If you outsmart the actuarians, however, you end up making money on the insurance company. As the insurers boast, you cannot outlive your annuity. If you die early, on the other hand, you lose your annuity. Here the company makes money and uses it to pay its longer-living annuitants.

There are several ways to hedge your bet in this annuity scheme. One option available in your annuity is called a *refund.* This election simply guarantees that either you or your beneficiary will be paid back at least the amount of money that you originally invested. For example, if you invest $100,000 in an annuity but die after only $60,000 has been paid out to you, a refund option would guarantee that your beneficiary would get the other $40,000. Having this option, however, would not prevent you from receiving more than $100,000 if you continue to live longer.

Another annuity variation is called a *years-certain* option, which guarantees you or your beneficiary payments for a minimum number of years or the length of your life, whichever is greater. Still another way of hedging your life-expectancy bet is something called a *joint-and-survivor annuity.* With this election the insurance company promises to pay either of two joint tenants as long as either is living.

All these options, of course, cost you money by reducing the interest paid compared to similar annuities without such options. But many annuitants find that only the promise of lifetime payments, plus a provision for their surviving spouse, provides the type of security that prompted them to buy the annuity in the first place.

Annuities for IRAs

Since IRAs are contributed to each year instead of being bought in a lump sum, the insurance companies have designed special installment annuities specifically for IRA plans. They are called *flexible-premium installment annuities.* The payments may be made monthly, quarterly, semiannually, or annually; and there is no minimum that must be paid each time.

Another annuity option that applies to this IRA installment plan is called a *waiver of premium.* This means that if you become disabled and cannot work, the insurance company will continue making your payments into your IRA account for you. Many IRA investors are choosing the waiver option as a type of insurance on their IRAs. Like the other annuity options, it isn't free; your investment yield will be reduced if you decide to take the waiver of premium.

Since there are three general investment choices with an IRA annuity, this annuity is said to have *flexible funding.* One investment choice is an interest-bearing account, called a *fixed-rate annuity.* The insurance company derives its income for this plan from real estate, mortgage, and bond investments and announces in the beginning of each year how much interest it will pay for that year. In the beginning of 1982, when IRAs first became available to everyone, insurance companies were "posting" annual rates as high as 15 percent, guaranteed for as long as two years. The 1983 rates were usually in the 10 percent range.

Some companies simply post *minimum rates* (around 6 percent for 1983) and promise to pay whatever amount over the minimum their investment portfolios produce. Another rate referred to in connection with the fixed-rate annuity is something called the *floor rate*. This is the minimum interest that the annuity will always pay for the life of the contract. This rate is simply a safety precaution and would come into play only in cases of extreme deflation. The 1983 floor rates are about 3 to 4 percent.

The second investment plan that you can choose for your IRA is called a *variable annuity*. This is simply a common stock fund, very similar to the ones offered by the mutual fund companies. And the third investment choice is a *money market fund*, now offered by most insurance companies.

You can switch from one investment vehicle to another within the same plan as often as you wish. If you spread your money out between two or more of the investment choices, you are using a strategy the insurance people call *split-funding*.

Although the IRA plans are designed to be *annuitized* after you retire, there is no obligation to do this. You can use an insurance plan to accumulate your IRA funds and then withdraw from this plan later when you retire. Conversely, you can accumulate your IRA funds somewhere else, then purchase an *immediate-pay annuity* when you retire. But once you start the annuitization itself, you're in it for life (and beyond, depending on your options).

Watch out for a number of fees in the annuity IRAs. Some companies charge a stiff *surrender fee* if you transfer your funds to another custodianship. This charge can be very high (up to 10 percent), although most companies drop the fee after your money has been in the plan for a certain number of years. There might even be a fee for switching your investment objectives—moving money from fixed income to the stock fund, for example. Some companies still charge a *front-load* commission, which can be as high as 8½ percent. Those that don't charge this fee make their profit from what's known as *the spread:* the difference between what they earn on your money and what they actually credit to your account. These are the companies that charge the surrender fee (also called *back-load*) in order to keep money in the accounts.

Advantages and Disadvantages

The insurance industry prides itself on the fact that it offers some unique features in its IRA plans. Two of the most beneficial are the opportunity for a guaranteed lifetime income and the optional guaranteed continuation of contributions (waiver of premium).

The main disadvantage of the insurance plans is their cost. Prudential, the nation's largest insurance company, takes 8¾ percent of each contribution and then charges small annual fees on top of that. Most companies have replaced this front-load with the back-load surrender fees. The way insurance companies compound interest is often unfavorable, too: annually instead of daily.

The investment choices between mutual funds and insurance companies are really not much different: fixed income, growth funds, and money market funds. The ramifications of each of these choices have been covered in previous chapters. With an insurance IRA, however, you have a plan that is designed to be eventually annuitized. You build up funds with the insurance company during the contributions stage and then buy a certain amount of guaranteed lifetime income with those funds after you retire. But your IRA funds need not accumulate in an insurance annuity, since you can buy that lifetime annuity anytime with a lump-sum payment.

Specific Plans

The table that follows capsulizes the IRA plans offered by several of the major insurance companies.

IRA Annuity Plans
Characteristics of Typical Life Insurance Companies

COMPANY	PRODUCTS OFFERED*	INTEREST RATES ON FIXED ANNUITY**	MINIMUMS		FEES			
			INITIAL	INCREMENT	FRONT-LOAD	ANNUAL INVESTMENT	TO SWITCH	BACK-LOAD***
Nationwide Life Ins. Co.	MMF Stocks Bonds	11¼%—2 yrs.	$300/ 1st year	None	None	$32.00	None	5%—0 for 8 yrs.
Kemper Ins. Co.	MMF Stocks Bonds	10½%—3 mo.	$25.00	$25.00	None	1.3% plus $25.00	None	6%—0 for 6 yrs.
Aetna Life & Casualty	MMF Stocks Bonds	9½% var.	$85/mo. or $1000/yr.	None	None	$20 plus .25%	None	5%—0 for 9 yrs.
Prudential Ins. Co.	Fixed Rate only	8½%—1 yr.	$15/mo.	None	None	$10.00	None	7%—0 for 11 yrs.

*Money market funds, stock funds, bond funds
**As of June 30, 1983.
***Withdrawal charges gradually decrease and are eliminated after a certain number of years.

12

Which Plan Is Best?

The question of which IRA plan is the best has to rival such recent topics as housing prices, the energy crisis, and balancing the budget as one of America's most common subjects of conversation.

There have been thousands of articles, lectures, and brochures on the subject of IRAs. There have been millions of advertisements for IRAs this year alone, in every form of media, each extolling the virtues of some sponsor. Yet there is no agreement as to which IRA is the best. Financial experts, business writers, and investment advisers each have their favorite plans. There are good arguments in favor of each custodian type, as you can see from the previous chapters in this section of the book. But of course there is no single plan, or even type of plan, that is best for all investors.

There are clearly some plans that are better than others within the same category. You can tell this from several of the tables in the previous chapters: mutual funds that have consistently outperformed their competition, brokerage firms that offer more products at lower fees, and depository and annuity plans that offer higher interest rates than their competition. Once you have decided what type of plan you want, the job of choosing the specific company is easier.

We spent much of this book getting acquainted with the different financial institutions that offer IRA plans. I wanted the reader to know exactly what he or she would get by going to a bank to open an IRA plan, for example, compared to going to a brokerage firm. As you know now, there are tremendous differences. As one of the ads announces: "Not all IRAs are created equal."

There *is* an answer, however, to the question of which type of IRA custodian is best *for you*, and I want to spend the rest of this chapter helping you decide.

Which one of the custodians you should go with, I feel, depends on seven factors, in this order of importance: your overall financial picture, your other retirement coverage, your investment objectives, the amount of risk you are willing to take, your age, your experience as an investor, and the amount of interest that you have in investing.

Let's take a look at each one of these factors and figure out where you fit in each category. This will determine which plan really is best for you.

Your Financial Picture

An evaluation of your financial situation should include more than just your income and your net worth. There are many other variables to consider. How stable is your income, for example? Does it change from year to year? How stable is your job? How much can the economy affect your job or your business? These are certainly things to think about if you are considering tying up money for the rest of your life.

How are you figuring your net worth? Cash in the bank can count a lot more than inflated real estate values, for example. How volatile and how liquid are your assets? What are the terms of your debts?

What sort of cash reserves do you have to meet emergencies or unexpected expenses? Are your family finances apt to change in the future? Is your spouse going to stop working? Are you getting married? Divorced? Do you have any large expenses coming up in the future, such as tuition, home purchase, or support of an older relative?

What other investments do you have now? How risky are they? Can you depend on their returning your principal at a certain time? What sort of financial discipline do you have: are you a saver or a spender?

These are all factors you must consider when determining your financial capability to put money into an IRA account for a long period of time.

Other Retirement Coverage

How important is your IRA to you as a retirement plan? For some people, an IRA will be the only source of retirement savings. Others, of course, are more than adequately covered by their own pension or Keogh plan; IRA will just be a tax deduction and supplementary investment account.

How good is your company pension plan? Are you already vested? Are you self-employed? Do you have a Keogh plan? If you are incorporated, you may already have a good retirement plan in the form of a pension or profit-sharing account.

What about an existing IRA plan? Many people have been eligible for IRAs since they began in 1975. If you are transferring an existing IRA plan to a new custodian or are rolling over funds out of a Keogh or pension plan into an IRA, then your investment choices will be much greater. Self-directed plans, for example, make much more sense for larger sums of money that have already accumulated in an existing retirement plan.

Try to rate your current retirement coverage within a range of having no other plan at all to being already adequately covered by an existing Keogh or pension plan.

Investment Objectives

Are you growth oriented or income oriented? There are good arguments for each approach. While growth may be the only possibility of beating inflation, risk-free income investments (such as money market funds) have been hard to beat in recent years with interest rates so high.

If you are going to look for growth, do you want to try for aggressive, shorter-term appreciation or gradual, longer-term appreciation?

If your objective is income, would you rather have a fixed return for a period of time or have your interest rate change continually with current rates?

You must decide what you want to accomplish before making any investment decision.

Risk Factor

How much risk are you willing to take to accomplish your financial goals? An insured certificate of deposit has no risk of principal at all, but it has no chance of increasing in value. A mutual fund that has growth potential of 25 percent per year, however, has to have some risk too. And a stock that can double in a year can also decline in value just as fast.

The depository institutions offer the safest yet least exciting places to harbor your retirement funds. High-quality growth funds with long-standing performance records offer good growth potential with relative safety. Individual securities bought through a self-directed plan offer the greatest potential along with the most risk.

Age

In general, the younger you are, the more growth and risk oriented you can afford to be. Not considering any of the other factors in this list for a moment, we could say that IRA investors in their twenties and thirties might look mostly for growth, while people in their forties and fifties should attempt to find a balanced plan, and those in their sixties should stay with the safest plans if they are just starting an IRA for the first time.

Of course, the age factor can easily be overshadowed by any of the other considerations here. There are certainly younger people who cannot afford any risk at all and older people who are more than willing to speculate completely with a few thousand dollars a year.

Investment Experience

How much experience do you already have with investing your money? Of the 100 million American workers suddenly eligible for IRAs this year, the majority of them have never put their money into anything but a checking account, savings account, or money market fund. The next largest group of IRA participants this year will be those with limited investment experience, having ventured small sums in a mutual fund or individual security. A relatively small percentage of these people will have already been exposed to the entire array of investment choices available to IRA accounts.

Interest in Investing

How involved do you want to be with your IRA? Some people love to follow the financial markets and want to handle all the decision making themselves. Others simply want to squirrel their money away each year and never think about it again. Fortunately there are both active investment vehicles and passive investment vehicles available for IRAs.

Which Type Are You?

Considering all these factors together, we should be able to come up with an answer to the question of which IRA plan is best for you. The following chart can be helpful if you find that you consistently fall into the same category for most of the factors that we just discussed.

While the majority of all people may fall into the most conservative category, there are certainly large numbers of people who can afford to be slightly more adventurous with their IRA plans.

Which IRA Plan Is Best for You?

	DEPOSITORY PLANS	MUTUAL FUNDS AND ANNUITIES	SELF-DIRECTED PLANS
Financial Picture	lower income, possibly high expenses, little reserves	stable and adequate income, cash reserves, good for discipline	high income, other investments, good liquidity
Other Retirement Coverage	no other plan	company pension, existing IRA	Keogh plan or own pension plan
Investment Objectives	dependable interest	long-term appreciation	more aggressive growth
Risk Factor	complete safety	some risk in return for growth potential	willing to take more risk to get greater performance
Age (several exceptions)	older	middle age	younger
Investment Experience	none	limited	have already invested in most types
Interest	don't want to think about it	interested, but believe in professional management	actively involved

The 100 Most Common Questions Asked About IRAs

13

Contributions

Q. *Do wage earners in all tax brackets qualify for an IRA?*

A. Yes. Although people in the higher brackets, since they pay the largest chunk of their income in taxes, will realize the greatest tax savings, IRAs are important for people in almost all tax brackets.

Q. *Must I work full time? Is there a minimum-hour requirement?*

A. No to both questions. Any employed person, no matter how limited the hours or the frequency or duration of employment, is eligible for an IRA. The only requirement is that you contribute earned income. With the unemployment rate currently at 9.5 percent, over 90 percent of adult Americans qualify for an IRA. This probably means you!

Q. *May I establish an IRA at any age?*

A. Legally you can establish an IRA and make contributions up until the last day of the year in which

165

you turn seventy and a half, provided that you are still employed and are contributing earned income. If you are approaching retirement, however, a long-term investment may not be appropriate.

On the other side of the age spectrm, for those precocious youngsters already focusing on comfortable retirement, there is no minimum age level. But then, most of us are unable to plan for financial contingencies two months down the road, not to mention fifty years!

Q. *What is the maximum allowable contribution?*

A. You can contribute $2000 annually to an individual IRA.

Q. *How do I provide for a nonworking spouse?*

A. You may establish an associated "spousal account" for your nonworking partner and contribute a maximum total of $2250 into the two accounts. There are no requirements as to how that money must be divided, as long as the contribution to either account does not exceed $2000.

Q. *Is there any limitation on the amount of income or growth that may increase the value of my IRA in a given year?*

A. No. The IRS is concerned only with the amount of money that you put in the account each year. Once that money has been contributed, you may make (or lose) as much as you want with it.

Q. *Must I contribute income that I actually earned this year to take a current year deduction?*

A. As long as you are contributing earned income or money that represented compensation for employment, it need not come from this year's earnings. Many people will probably be funding their IRAs with money taken from past savings in an attempt to put that essentially idle (and taxable) money to better use.

Q. *Can I fund my IRA in any way with unearned income?*

A. No. Gifts, inheritance, and lucky sweeps at the track are all outside the realm of IRAs. Congratulate yourself on your unexpected windfall but find another vehicle to shelter that money.

Q. *Can I contribute earned income from foreign-based sources?*

A. No, you may only contribute earned income on which you would normally pay US federal income tax.

Q. *Is there a minimum contribution?*

A. No, although some plans may specify their own annual minimum.

Q. *Must I contribute annually to an established IRA?*

A. No. You may skip your contribution altogether in any year that you want.

Q. *If I am unable to contribute my own money in a given year, can I contribute money that is earned by another individual, and let that person take the tax deduction?*

A. No, although that would admittedly work out well for both of you: you get the money into your account earning tax-free income, and someone else gets a write-off. Unfortunately it's not exactly satisfactory to the IRS. IRAs are set up for the benefit of only one person, and so you may contribute to and deduct from only one account in only one name.

Q. *Can I borrow money to fund an IRA if I am eligible but financially unable to contribute?*

A. Yes, you can. And you can deduct the cost of your loan.

Q. *How do contribution requirements apply to spousal accounts when both spouses are not the same age?*

A. No contribution can be made into either account when the working spouse reaches seventy and a half. If the nonworking spouse turns seventy and a half first, no further contributions can be made to that account, but the working spouse can still contribute to his or her own account until age seventy and a half.

Q. *In any given year can I make a contribution into a spousal account solely for the benefit of one of us?*

A. Yes, as long as it does not exceed $2000.

Q. *What is the deadline for establishing an IRA?*

A. IRAs must be established and funded each year by the tax filing date, April 15, for the previous year's deduction. If you obtain a filing extension, your IRA contribution deadline is similarly extended. However, your custodian may ask to see the IRS letter granting that extension before accepting your contribution. Note that if you file early you must also make your contribution early, to correspond with your filing date. You can't deduct something you haven't paid for yet!

Q. *What is the optimum time of year to contribute to my IRA?*

A. The earlier the better. The sooner you can anticipate your annual income and commit the funds to your retirement, the sooner that money can accumulate and compound tax free.

Q. *Must my annual contribution be a lump sum or can I spread out payments during the course of the year?*

A. A lump-sum payment at the beginning of the year would provide optimum tax advantage by getting your money quickly into a sheltered environment. The difference in accumulated income from a contribution made early in January and one made at the last minute is significant, as illustrated earlier in the book (see page 69, Contribution Deadlines).

It may not always be possible to make a single payment, especially at the beginning of the year. And for those whose contribution may be significantly less than the legal maximum, storing away $10 or $25 a week may be the only way to ensure that the funds designated for retirement will actually end up in an IRA. Here your company's payroll-deduction plan may be the best thing. See page 99 for examples of how small contributions build up.

Q. *Can I establish a withdrawal plan from my checking so that funds are automatically transferred to my IRA?*

A. Yes. Check with your bank and your custodian for the specific procedure.

Q. *Can my employer sponsor an IRA on my behalf so that I can make payroll deductions to the plan?*

A. Yes, this is possible and it is undeniably convenient. But as already suggested, such a plan will result in contributions still being made late in the year, when it would be much more advantageous to be sheltering the money earlier in the year. Review Chapter 6 on employer-related IRAs.

Q. Can I specify how much I want my employer to deduct from each paycheck, or is it predetermined by my salary?

A. You set the amount, as long as the total contribution from your year's deductions does not exceed $2000. The IRS has abolished the percentage-of-income limitation, so you may contribute up to 100 percent of your income provided that it does not exceed the maximum.

Q. May I have more than one IRA?

A. Yes, as long as the combined total contribution does not exceed the maximum allowed.

Q. Can I contribute securities I already own?

A. No, you may only contribute cash to your IRA. Assets not in that form are considered property and as such are prohibited from IRA contributions. You may, however, contribute the cash redeemed from securities you own. In a self-directed plan you may use these proceeds to repurchase the same security.

Q. When must I stop making contributions?

A. You must stop contributing at age 70½ or when you stop working, whichever is earlier.

Q. What happens to my IRA if I stop working, assuming that I am still financially able to make contributions?

A. Regardless of your financial position, once you stop working you are no longer eligible to contribute to your IRA. You may, however, continue to manage it. You may resume making contributions—or establish a new IRA—when you return to work, as long as you have not reached age 70½.

Q. Can I resume making contributions if I return to work after I have begun withdrawing funds?

A. You may resume making contributions provided it meets with the rules of the plan established by your custodian. You can always start another IRA and continue withdrawing from your original IRA while making contributions to the new plan, or simply transfer the original funds into an investment that allows additional contributions.

Q. *Is it conceivable that between the ages of 59½ and 70½ I might be making contributions to and receiving distributions from my IRA simultaneously?*

A. Yes, you may wish to continue your contributions while withdrawing funds to take advantage of the tax write-off each year. Here, again, check with your custodian; some may not allow you to do this without a fee.

Q. *Does a two-income couple filing jointly establish one or two IRAs?*

A. Each working spouse is eligible to establish his or her own IRA, for a total contribution of $4000, regardless of whether they file jointly or singly. There is no such thing as a *joint* IRA.

Q. *If I intend to file a joint return, must both my spouse and I have IRAs? Can one of us make contributions to an IRA in just one name?*

A. You can certainly have just one IRA. However, there is no reason *not* to set up two IRAs if you both work, or a spousal account if only one of you is employed, if you can afford it.

Q. *Can I overcontribute in one year to compensate for an undercontribution in a preceding year? Can I undercontribute to make up for an overcontribution?*

A. An overcontribution in any year is hit with a 6 percent penalty (see page 68), even if you have con-

tributed less than the maximum in a previous year.
You may undercontribute in a given year to make
up for a previous overcontribution, but this will not
excuse you from the 6 percent penalty during the
year or years that you carried the overcontribution.

Q. *Will contributions to an IRA have any effect on the
distribution of Social Security payments upon my
retirement?*

A. Assuming that the Social Security program is still
around when you reach retirement, your IRA
would simply supplement those payments. (See
Chapter 1 on the Social Security system's problems.)

Q. *How many times per year can I contribute to my
IRA account?*

A. The IRS does not limit the number of contributions
as long as the total amount does not exceed $2000.
Your specific plan, however, may have its own
limitations on number of contributions.

Q. *May I continue contributing to my ex-wife's or ex-
husband's spousal account?*

A. No. Spousal accounts do not apply to former
spouses. The IRS does not recognize couples who
are legally separated under a divorce decree as being still married. In addition, for tax purposes the
IRS determines marital status as of the last day of
the tax year; if you contribute to a spousal account
in May and then divorce in November, your contribution will be considered an overcontribution subject to the 6 percent penalty.

Q. *What happens to a spousal account when the
spouse for whom is was established becomes employed?*

A. You may no longer contribute to or claim a deduction for your spouse's IRA during any tax year in which your spouse earned any income. Newly employed spouses may establish their own accounts and make contributions based on their own incomes.

Q. *May I roll over a lump-sum distribution (from another retirement plan) into several different IRA plans?*

A. Yes. The IRS has no limit on the number of IRAs that can accept a rollover. (See Chapter 6 on rollovers.)

Q. *What is the difference between a rollover and a transfer?*

A. A *rollover* is the taking of retirement funds out of a pension, profit-sharing, or Keogh plan and putting them in an IRA plan, when you retire or change jobs. An IRA *transfer* is just a matter of switching funds from one IRA plan to another. (See Chapter 5, Changing Your Mind, on IRA transfers.)

Q. *Can I roll over just part of my retirement fund into an IRA and retain the other portion for personal use?*

A. Yes, the IRS now allows partial rollovers.

14

Tax
Considerations

Q. *What are the tax benefits of an IRA?*

A. Very simply, IRAs function in two ways: They reduce your immediate tax outlay and they provide an environment where your income and capital gains can accumulate and compound untaxed until they are withdrawn. In this tax-deferred environment your funds will grow at a much faster rate than they would after being taxed. When your money is finally withdrawn at retirement—when your income is likely to be reduced—it may be taxed at a lower rate.

Q. *How do I achieve the greatest tax advantage from my IRA?*

A. Make the maximum allowable contribution, make your contribution as soon after January 1 as possible, and invest your money wherever you can obtain the highest return.

Q. *How can I figure my annual tax savings resulting from my IRA contribution?*

A. Just multiply your contribution by your tax bracket. Remember that you pay taxes on marginal or incremental income—the "last dollar" above a basic figure—so your bracket may be higher than you think. (Refer to pages 63–65 for tax tables and an explanation of brackets.)

   Someone in the 35 percent bracket would realize a net tax savings of $700 on a $2000 contribution; someone in the 50 percent bracket would realize a $1000 net savings on the same contribution.

Q. *How do I report the status of my IRA to the IRS? Are there specific forms I must file with my tax return?*

A. You need merely list your deduction on line 25 of Form 1040 as an "adjustment to gross income." (See page 62 for Form 1040.) Form 5329 ("Return for Individual Retirement Arrangement Taxes") is required only to report overcontributions, undercontributions, or premature distributions and any associated penalty tax.

Q. *Must I report to the IRS any IRA to which I did not contribute during the tax filing year?*

A. No.

Q. *Can I contribute to an IRA and claim a tax reduction if my income level would not otherwise require me to file a tax return?*

A. Yes. The continuing tax protection of your contribution could be beneficial in the future.

Q. *Will the custodian of my IRA report to the government?*

A. Yes, your custodian must report annually on the

status of your account, including any interest or dividend income generated as well as any penalties assessed.

Q. Since the government evidently encourages providing for one's own retirement needs, is there any way that I can avail myself of the allowed tax deduction without actually contributing to an IRA plan?

A. No. You are not entitled to any deduction unless you make a contribution.

Q. Is it conceivable that future changes in IRS regulations would retroactively alter the tax-deferred status of my IRA?

A. The IRS will update and amend IRA regulations to suit the needs of the country's work force. However, such changes would generally govern only future contribution and eligibility requirements. Your custodian is obligated to disclose the effects of any new regulations that could affect you and your investment. (See page 25, Helping Yourself, on proposed IRA revision.)

Q. Briefly, what are the regulations that I need to know to avoid incurring any penalties?

A. 1. The legal maximum annual contribution is $2000, or $2250 for the inclusion of a nonworking spouse. Excesses are subject to ordinary income tax and assessed a 6 percent penalty each year until removed from the account.
2. You may contribute up to the year in which you become 70½ or whenever you stop working, whichever is earlier. Contributions continued beyond that are subject to the 6 percent overcontribution penalty and possibly a 50 percent underdistribution penalty (see #4).

3. Any funds withdrawn before you reach 59½ are considered premature and are taxed as ordinary income in addition to a 10 percent penalty tax.

4. You must begin receiving distributions by the year in which you turn 70½. At that time if you withdraw less than the minimum scheduled amount, you will be subject to a 50 percent penalty on the portion of the specified amount that is not withdrawn. (See Chapter 5 on IRA penalties.)

Q. *How will any penalties be assessed?*

A. You must add any penalties to your federal income tax and file Form 5329 with your tax return.

Q. *Do overcontributions or undercontributions affect my tax-deferred status?*

A. No. You will be assessed a penalty, but there are no consequences on the overall tax status of your account.

Q. *How can I avoid the 6 percent overcontribution penalty?*

A. By withdrawing the excess amount before your tax filing date, you will not be subject to the excess tax.

Q. *If I have bought securities with an overcontribution and the assets have depreciated in value to within the legal maximum, will I still be penalized? How much must I actually withdraw to bring my contribution to the allowed amount?*

A. You must withdraw the dollar amount equivalent to your original overcontribution, regardless of the current value. However, the 6 percent overcontribution penalty will be assessed only on the value of the overcontribution as of the end of the year, so you will be taxed on the depreciated value.

Q. *How much of my contribution is tax deductible?*

A. One hundred percent of your contribution is tax deductible, provided that you have observed the contribution limitations.

Q. *If my IRA contains stocks or bonds, will losses in value incurred be tax deductible?*

A. No, because you are already receiving a substantial tax break. You can't deduct something more than once. Additionally, your IRA funds will be taxed at the ordinary income rate upon distribution, so you needn't temper your investment strategies for fear of capital-gains tax. (See Chapter 7, Income vs. Growth, for a discussion of gains and losses.)

Q. *If my contribution is too small to allow me to itemize my deductions on my tax return, will the IRS still recognize the tax status of my IRA?*

A. Absolutely. IRA investments are deducted from gross earnings, so your eligibility or personal choice to itemize has no bearing on your IRA.

Q. *In the case of a spousal IRA, must the same spouse who contributes to the IRA also claim the tax deduction?*

A. If you're filing jointly, it's a moot point. For those filing two separate returns, the spouse into whose account the contribution is made must claim the deduction on his or her return. This underscores the principle that the nonworking spouse's account is separate and distinct from the working spouse's; and contributions, once made, are nontransferable.

Q. *Will I lose any tax advantage in rolling funds into another IRA?*

A. No, not if you adhere to the legal requirements and those established specifically by your custodian.

Always check for transfer or termination charges with your custodian and remember that you will probably incur additional fees to set up a new IRA. (See Chapter 5, Changing Your Mind, on IRA transfers.)

Q. *Am I required to keep IRA records for a minimum length of time?*

A. The IRS states that you must keep all records pertinent to the administration of any IRS law. If at all feasible, plan on keeping your IRA records indefinitely. If that sounds impossible, strive at least to maintain accurate records for the life of the plan.

Q. *Do tax regulations differ for employer-sponsored IRAs?*

A. No.

Q. *Can I use my IRA as collateral for a loan?*

A. The IRS strictly prohibits this use of IRAs, because such a use would represent actively using funds that are meant to be untouched until retirement. Any amount used as collateral is therefore considered a premature withdrawal and will be taxed as such.

Q. *Do creditors have any claim to the funds in my IRA?*

A. Your IRA is out of the reach of creditors in some states, such as California, but not in most.

Q. *Will state and local taxes be affected by my IRA contribution?*

A. To the dismay of most taxpayers, there is no single answer that applies to every state. Check with your local IRS office to determine your state's and municipality's interpretation and application of IRA tax deductions.

Q. *I've heard both "tax-free" and "tax-deferred" used in reference to IRAs; which is accurate?*

A. In the strict sense of the word, IRAs are tax-deferred; you will pay taxes eventually, after the funds are withdrawn from your plan. Your tax bracket may be lower in retirement than during your working years, so when you do pay taxes, it should be at a reduced rate (although both principal and interest will be taxed as ordinary income then).

15

Investing

Q. *What types of IRA plans currently exist to accommodate my retirement needs?*

A. Various plans are offered by banks, S & Ls, credit unions, insurance companies, mutual funds, and brokerage firms. With the exception of certain investments, you can invest in most of the same vehicles offered by these institutions for non-IRA accounts.

Q. *What type of investment should I avoid?*

A. Avoid tax-advantaged investments. Municipal (tax-free) bonds, for example, are not logical, because you don't need to shelter an investment that's already sheltered. And once it is in an IRA, tax-free bond income actually becomes taxable upon withdrawal.

Q. *Are some investments safer than others?*

A. Of course; the degree of risk is directly related to the return you can expect. Your IRA is only as safe as the investments that are in it. And even within a category of investments, the quality of management and performance of each specific plan varies greatly. (See Section III for comparisons of IRA plans.)

Q. *Is there a plan in which I can manage my own money and determine the course of my investment?*

A. Yes. Brokerage firms offer self-directed plans that give you the freedom to manage your portfolio as you see fit. Neither commodities nor margin trading is permitted, and you will incur brokerage commissions on every transaction, but the IRA shelter does give you an opportunity to trade your securities without concern for short-term capital gains taxes. The fees for this account will be considerably higher than for most other IRAs, so it should only be considered by those wishing to participate actively with an IRA and take advantage of the extensive investment opportunities.

Q. *Is it strategically sound to diversify with several investments?*

A. The thought behind it is good, but the reality is that $2000 parlayed into several different investments is impractical. You simply cannot stretch $2000 very effectively into more than a couple of investments and hope to see results. You can, however, diversify by investing in a mutual fund or an insurance annuity. (See Section III for more information.)

Q. *Does an IRA conflict with any other retirement plan?*

A. No. IRAs may be used in conjunction with other plans to supplement your retirement nest egg. A person with a pension plan or Keogh, for example, can also contribute annually to an IRA.

Q. *Are there other types of tax-sheltered investments I could use as effectively as an IRA to plan for my retirement?*

A. Yes. Depending on your needs and circumstances, there are a variety of investments that will permit you to defer taxes until retirement. Someone with a very high income, for instance, might be better suited to an investment that is not restricted to a $2000 annual contribution. Your tax specialist or accountant will be able to direct you further on the basis of your specific requirements and objectives (See the discussion What's Better Than IRAs? beginning on page 51.)

Q. *Typically, what are the fees associated with IRA plans?*

A. Even similar plans vary considerably, so be cautious. Generally, banks and savings and loans are the least expensive and brokerage firms and insurance companies the most expensive. Some plans charge only a one-time setup fee, others a flat maintenance fee, others a management fee based on your net asset value, and still others some combination. Some fees are levied up front, others throughout the life of the investment, and others when you take money out. So know what you're getting into. Don't be surprised fifteen years down the road! (See Section III for complete coverage of fees for each custodian. The tables on pages 90, 106, 141, 142–43, and 154 summarize typical plan fees.)

Q. *Are the fees (initial fees, maintenance fees, commissions) included in the maximum allowable annual contribution?*

A. Although there is still no IRS ruling on this question, IRA expenses are generally considered deductible (under Miscellaneous on your tax return) separately and in addition to your IRA contribution limits.

Q. Are there restrictions on the type of assets allowed in an IRA?

A. Yes. The IRS does not allow precious metals, coins, artwork, or other assets usually termed as "collectibles." In addition, IRA investments cannot be financed in any way with leverage or debt. Although commodity futures are allowed by the IRS, most brokerage firms will not accept them (except through a managed commodity fund) in a self-directed IRA because of the risk.

Q. Can I purchase real estate in my IRA?

A. Real estate is approved for IRAs but generally avoided because the $2000 contribution ceiling seriously limits the investment potential. There are, however, real estate partnerships designed specifically for IRA accounts (See page 123, Real Estate Partnerships.)

Q. Are insurance companies approved as IRA custodians, or must I establish an insurance plan via a bank custodial account?

A. Provided that the company has a prototype insurance plan that meets IRS specifications, it can legally function as your IRA custodian.

Q. Can I purchase either whole-life or term insurance?

A. No.

Q. What type of insurance investments qualify for an IRA?

A. There are numerous annuity plans that qualify for IRAs. (See Chapter 11, Insurance Company Plans, for more information.)

Q. If my annuity is set up with an annual premium cost that is less than my allowable IRA tax deduction, can I apply the difference toward another IRA investment?

A. Yes, you may contribute the difference between the legal maximum contribution and the deductible portion of your premium via another IRA investment. For example, if your annual premium is $1000, $900 of which goes into retirement savings, you could invest the remaining $1100 in another IRA plan.

Q. *Will I be able to designate how much of my annuity premium should go to retirement savings? How else will I know what I can legally deduct?*

A. The custodian of your contract will provide a statement that breaks down the taxable and tax-deductible components of the plan, which are all fixed in each plan.

Q. *Can I designate the insurance annuity I already own as an IRA?*

A. No; it would have to have been originally established as an IRA plan.

Q. *Must I take distribution of my insurance IRA in a lump-sum payment?*

A. No; you may elect to spread out the distributions in periodic payments beginning no later than the year in which you reach 70½.

Q. *If I invest in a time-defined vehicle, such as a CD, must I adhere to maturity dates of the investment despite my eligibility to begin receiving distributions?*

A. Yes. The IRS regulations on contributions and withdrawals are the legal guidelines, but many institutions and investments maintain more specific requirements. Familiarize yourself with the rules concerning your plan to avoid being subject to penalties. (CDs, incidentally, normally waive the early-withdrawal penalty if the investor is retiring.)

Q. *How does compounding affect the yield?*

A. The more frequent the compounding, the higher the yield. Compounding can be done on a daily, a quarterly, semiannual, or annual basis; over the long run the differences in total yield can be significant. (See page 94 on compounding.)

Q. *Is there any guarantee that my funds are actually protected and insured until retirement?*

A. That depends on the investment vehicle and the institution backing it. Banks and S & Ls insure funds under the FDIC and FSLIC respectively for $100,000. (To avoid exposing your assets to lack of coverage, simply open up identical investments in different institutions when your IRA reaches $100,000.) Note that money market funds do not carry insurance coverage.

Q. *Is there any impartial agency to help me compare and rate various IRA plans?*

A. The IRS, the Federal Trade Commission (FTC), and the Pension Benefit Guarantee Corporation (a government agency) all have this kind of information.

Q. *Are the rules and regulations spelled out in a written agreement that I must sign?*

A. There is no such contract with the IRS. You will be required to sign an agreement with your custodian, however, stipulating the conditions of your particular plan, which is the only distinction between your IRA and the same investment in a non-IRA account.

Q. *Can I establish and maintain my IRA by mail?*

A. Generally, yes. Check with your custodian.

Q. *May I switch IRAs from one custodian to another?*

A. You may transfer your IRA directly to another custodian as often as you wish, provided the custodians involved are willing to accommodate your
whims. You may also make an indirect transfer
once a year (where you take possession of your IRA
funds and redeposit them with another custodian
within sixty days). Remember, though, that your
IRA is a retirement savings plan, and frequent
switching is not really consonant with the long-
term objective. Also, there are many institutions
that offer a choice of investments without requiring
a transfer in custodian. (See page 64, Changing
Your Mind.)

16

Distributions

Q. When may I legally begin to receive distributions?

A. You may begin withdrawing funds any time after you turn 59½; you must begin receiving distributions no later than the year that you become 70½. Between 59½ and 70½ you may withdraw as much or as little as you need or desire. After age 70½ you must take at least certain minimum distributions, which are dictated by the IRS's actuarial tables based on your life expectancy. (See page 70 for the IRS actuarial table.)

Q. Are there legal circumstances in which I could withdraw funds before the age of 59½?

A. If you are medically proven to be mentally or physically disabled and therefore unable to continue in any form of gainful employment, you may receive distributions without penalty at any time.

Q. Are funds distributed from a spousal account jointly or individually?

A. Funds are distributed separately, according to individual age and account value. Distributions need not begin in each spouse's account until the owner of that account reaches 70½, irrespective of which is the working and which is the nonworking spouse.

Q. *If I originally elected to receive periodic distributions, can I later choose to receive the remaining funds in a lump-sum payment?*

A. Yes.

Q. *Can I reinvest my IRA distribution directly in another tax-shelter vehicle?*

A. You can reinvest the distributed funds as you wish, but you must first pay the income tax due Uncle Sam.

Q. *Whom can I assign as beneficiary?*

A. There are no IRS restrictions concerning the designation of beneficiary.

Q. *Must an IRA beneficiary report to the IRS at all?*

A. Yes; as long as there are still funds in the account, its status must be reported to the IRS. You must file in any tax year during which there were funds in the account.

Q. *What happens to my IRA if I divorce?*

A. Each spouse's IRA contributions are separate. The working spouse—even though it was his or her income that funded the IRA—usually has no legal claim to the other's account. Spousal accounts can voluntarily be used as part of a divorce settlement, however, and in some states an IRA can be declared part of a settlement that is contested in court.

Only in the case of divorce can a spousal account exist independently of its source account (and then only if the account was opened five years prior to the divorce and funded during at least three of those years). Then the nonworking spouse may continue to make contributions from alimony, up to $1125 annually. If that spouse begins working, he or she can open a new account and/or continue to contribute to the existing account for a combined total of $2000.

Q. *What happens to my IRA in the event of death?*

A. If your beneficiary is your spouse, he or she may continue the tax deferral of your IRA by assuming ownership of the plan. A nonspouse beneficiary must now (staring in 1984) withdraw all inherited IRA funds within five years and pay income tax on it as it is paid out.

Q. *What about federal estate tax for beneficiaries?*

A. Spouse beneficiaries are now exempt from all estate tax. Nonspouse beneficiaries are subject to estate tax on amounts above certain exemption limits: $100,000 in 1983, but increasing over the next three years.